christmas

chRistMAS

new ideas for an old-fashioned celebration

BARBARA AND NADIA ROSENTHAL

Clarkson N. Potter, Inc./Publishers

DISTRIBUTED BY CROWN PUBLISHERS, INC. NEW YORK

Printed in the United States of America

Published simultaneously in Canada
by General Publishing Company Limited

Library of Congress Cataloging in Publication Data

Rosenthal, Barbara L.
    Christmas: new ideas for an old-fashioned celebration.
    Bibliography: p.
    Includes index.
    1. Christmas. I. Rosenthal, Nadia.
II. Title.
GT4985.R67   1980   394.2'68282   79-28665
ISBN: 0-517-536951

10 9 8 7 6 5 4 3 2 1
First Edition
    We gratefully acknowledge permission to reprint the following: "Pear
Chutney" from *A Taste of the Country* by Pamela Westland and "Maria's
Seville Marmalade" from *Cooking in Season* by Christine Brady reprinted
by permission of Hamish Hamilton Ltd., publishers.

Permissions continued on page 188.

Contents

The Winter Solstice   *page 11*

THE PREPARATION

1   **Beginning in the Summer**   *page 19*

Toys

The Summer Workshop   *page 26*

*Potpourri, Dried Flower Pictures, Shells as Presents,
Shell Pictures*

2   **Into the Autumn**   *page 35*

Cooked Presents

Special Shopping for Handmade Things

Mail-Order Shopping

3   **Advent: The Coming of Christmas**   *page 57*

The Christmas Factory   *page 60*

*Calendars, The Christmas Walnut, Covered Boxes,
Sachets, Shoe Mice, Embroidered Handkerchiefs and
Monogrammed Sheets, Making a Doll*

Christmas Cooking and Baking   *page 77*

*Christmas Meats, Fruitcakes, My Grandmother's
Christmas Cookies, Debra's Christmas Cookies,
Nadia's Christmas Cookies, Candies*

Decorating the House   *page 91*

*The Christmas Tree, To Make a Rose,
To Make a Wreath*

Wrapping Christmas Presents   *page 101*

THE CELEBRATION

4 Christmas Eve   *page 105*
    Putting Lights on the Tree
    Trimming the Tree
    Menu and Recipes
    The Night Before Christmas, Clement Clarke Moore

5 Christmas Day   *page 117*
    Menu and Recipes
    Carols
    Conversation About Christmas, Dylan Thomas

6 Christmas Week   *page 163*
    Boxing Day Menu and Recipes
    The Christmas Week Party
    Punches and Christmas Drinks
    Recipes for Christmas Week
    The New Year Menu and Recipes

7 Twelfth Night   *page 175*
    Menu and Recipes

Putting Things Away   *page 186*

    Bibliography   *page 189*

    Index of Recipes   *page 191*

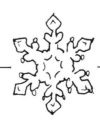

And the rites are in time what the home is in space
... Thus I walk from fête to fête,
from anniversary to anniversary,
from grape harvest to grape harvest,
as I walked, yet a child,
from the Council Chamber to the chamber of rest
... in the depths of my father's palace,
where every footstep has a meaning.

ANTOINE DE SAINT-EXUPÉRY

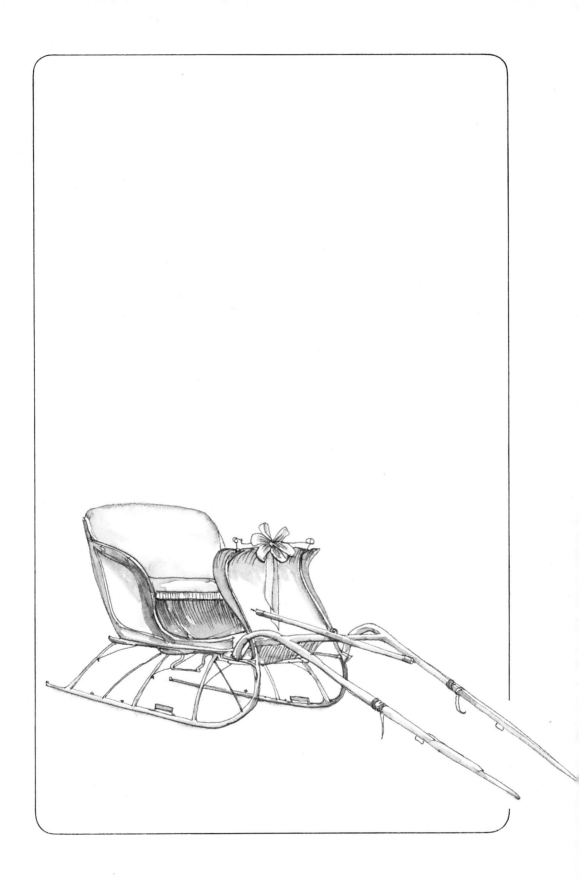

The Winter Solstice

The evolution of our personal family Christmas celebration began in my childhood and has grown into a full-blown production that is almost year-long in preparation. I am the producer of the event. I keep a red leather loose-leaf notebook to help remember everything, and Christmas still begins in July, as it did when our two daughters were little girls.

The drive from New York City to Maine, where we have our summer house, used to take ten to twelve hours, a long time for children or grownups. One year the top blew off our old Buick convertible (it was raining), and that was diverting. And one year our younger daughter became a radio, broadcasting outrageous programs for hours.

But the most engrossing of our pastimes evolved into a ritual, the beginning of one of the year's biggest rituals: the celebration of the winter solstice—Christmas. We made our Christmas lists. One list was a "realistic" list, and one a list of dreams—no holds barred. The nature of those lists is evoked by my elder daughter's first Christmas wish: a box of ribbons. A few years ago I gave her another box of ribbons, now to tie around her large-brimmed hats. These list-making times took up several hours of that long trip, and they were serious business. We each asked ourselves, "What do I want?" A trip to Bali to hear the gamelans, for Papa; a Rolls-Royce Silver Cloud with Chanel suits hanging in it for me; a palomino horse and a new flute case for Maria; a big set of gouaches for Nadia, and "a boat to sail away in." Dreams or realities?

We've all grown up now and when we are together we still do our Christmas lists on the way to Maine. And Christmas still begins in July. Even when we are opening the summer house, I know that there will be a day in late August that is the beginning of autumn. The knowing is in the feel of the wind and the smell of it, and the faith in nature's cyclical, spiraling progression. My memory returns to a Christmas Eve of my childhood in a mountain valley of western Pennsylvania. I was looking out

of the window, snowflakes were falling and the awe that filled me then fills me still. And one Christmas morning, very early, sitting alone with the glittering, magical Christmas tree, nibbling a piece of fudge for breakfast, there was that same awe.

There are other memories. The Christmas Eve my tuxedoed father, very merry from eggnog, fell into the coal bin while stoking the furnace of our house; the Christmas packages that arrived for me (by way of "Parsley Post"), from the Ohio and Maryland branches of my family, stacked on the ruby-red mohair-covered dining room chairs. I picked the corners of those packages all month, and once, only once, one Tuesday afternoon when my mother was at her weekly bridge club I opened one and retied it, and never told. My mother made mincemeat from the deer my father shot each year, and German Christmas cookies that had to age in their tins, and closer to Christmas the exquisite sand tarts, delicately decorated with colored sugars and almonds. There was the absolute certainty that Santa Claus's sleigh and reindeer would land on our roof, and down the chimney he would come to decorate the tree and leave the presents: the cream-colored bicycle so desired, the Lightning sled that is still mine (repainted by Nadia in bright colors a few years ago as my renewed present), my Shirley Temple doll (she lives now in the house in Maine) and Mary-Lou, who cried when you pressed her tummy (also living in Maine, but she has lost her cry).

At this moment in our history there is overpopulation, the lowering of standards, the rape of our jewellike planet, the end of romance and so on and so on. Yet when I tell friends that I am writing a book about celebration, the celebration of Christmas, there is an enthusiastic exchange about customs, why we do it and the joy of it. At lunch recently a friend of mine, living near London on an island in the Thames, told me that Christmas among the island families begins at his house with orange juice and champagne—Buckshots he called them; I call them Mimosas. There is a present for everyone, but these are the rules: the presents must be hanging on the tree, and no present may cost more than fifty pence. All day long the group of friends moves from one home to another—with more presents hanging on trees for all. Stuart spoke of the great fun in finding presents for one dollar, and the ingenuity and planning involved.

Again and again I find people who care how the ornaments and lights are put on their trees, who spend hours assembling trains and villages, making their own wreaths and wrapping presents with all the artistry of professional artists. Perhaps things aren't as bad as they seem so long as there are a few souls here and there who maintain a childlike enthusiasm for such times as Christmas and who love an elegant performance.

My daughters say that their stability as adults comes from the rituals of their childhood—Christmas, Easter, Summer, Halloween, Thanksgiving, Birthdays, St. Valentine's Day. They were full-scale productions. Now that we are all grown up we aren't together for most of these times. But Christmas is reunion time and the ritual is renewed each year. Larry is in charge of the lights for the tree and the outdoor lights, bringing the tree into the house and finding its "right side" (usually an occasion for a family battle royal). Nadia is his helper and she usually decorates the house. Maria bakes the *Christollen*. The roles shift and change, but I am always the producer and my lists and notes are voluminous, choking the red notebook and filling those days of my life with their execution.

Nadia made this entry in the red notebook last Christmas for the next year:

Don't let guests put trimmings on the tree without a Rosenthal in charge of handing out ornaments so that things go on right (e.g., 3 little angels should go together, discs need to be opened out, birdie's wings need spreading, etc.)

Also in the red notebook there is an old letter to Santa which I've kept:

Dear Santa,

The colored stocking is Maria's and the gray one is mine. Have a little snack from the kitchen—smoked salmon, caviar, champagne—anything you want!

XXX's
Nadia

I have my grandmother's German Christmas cookie recipes on yellowed pages neatly typed by my mother, and I beg and plead for some forest-shot venison for mincemeat from the local butcher and for a hand-plucked turkey. I collect things all year long for presents to give and hope to be organized for once. Fortunately it never happens, for I really prefer a "sensitive chaos" and part of the fun is scrambling to make it.

Rituals have come into being in all societies to mark the big moments of life: birth, initiation, marriage, death, and to help ensure fertility, a good harvest, the coming of spring, midsummer and the winter solstice. Winter has long been a time for feasting and celebration. Perhaps the hostility of the elements in northern climates caused men to be more conscious of their essential brotherhood. There were long nights to be filled and finally, when the days began to lengthen, there was the celebration of the return of the sun, the winter solstice.

The earliest known winter festival was the Sacaea in Babylon, a New Year celebration in which the king impersonated the god Marduk who had won a mighty victory over Tiamat, the goddess of Chaos, thus marking the very first New Year's Day. Many of the characteristics of the Sacaea celebration—feasting, disguising, changing roles from master to slave and vice versa —are to be found in ensuing winter festivals.

In Rome the twenty-fifth of December was celebrated as the *Dies Natalia Invieti Selis* (Birthday of the Unconquered Sun). This day was sacred to Mithras, the God of Light, and to Attis, the Phrygian Sun God. The Roman Saturnalia was a time of anarchy with wild merrymaking, outlandish dress, grotesque behavior and reversal of social place. It was a festival of fire and light that began on the seventeenth of December, continued for seven days, and was immediately followed by the New Year

celebration of Kalends. In the fourth century A.D. the Sophist Libanius described the winter festival in Antioch:

> There is food everywhere, heavy, rich food. And laughter. A positive urge to spend seizes on everyone, so that people who have taken pleasure in saving up the whole year now think it's a good idea to squander. The streets are full of people and coaches, staggering under the load of gifts. Children are free of the dread of their teachers, and for slaves the festival is as good as a holiday. Another good thing about it—it teaches people not to be too fond of money, but to let it circulate from hand to hand.

In northern Europe in icy winter the solstice celebration was called the festival of Yule. Evergreens were brought into the houses, gifts were made and blazing fires built to the dark gods Odin and Thor.

The early church fathers, who were looking for a day to celebrate Christ's birth and win converts to the new religion, chose a season of established festivals belonging to the pagan peoples of both north and south: Romans, Norsemen, Celts and Teutons. The celebrations were variously called Yule, Saturnalia, Kalends. In the twentieth century, Christmas remains an astonishing creation: a pagan festival, a midwinter romp, an extraordinary combination of the sacred and burlesque and a curious blend of Christian and pagan symbolism.

Renewal is a constant part of nature's process; I wonder if ritual is Time's renewal. I think of the Christmas season, the winter solstice, as the resolution (re-solution) and therefore the renewal of the year, the defeat of the goddess of Chaos and her rebirth into a "sensitive chaos." In our collective unconscious there is a deep connection to the elements and to nature. We are part of nature's sequence and progression. Our response to the sun's renewal may or may not be conscious, but respond we do. Special times—holidays, either sacred or secular—give a moment of pause in the flow of life, an exhalation, time to take stock, to muse. Children return to the home; friends gather. But past all the words there is the awe in our natures that celebrates itself at the winter solstice: a time of magic, Christmas.

the
PREPARATION

Meandering leads to perfection.

LAO-TSE
(c. 604–531 B.C.)

1

Beginning in the Summer

In the skin at the tips of our fingers
we see the trail of the wind.
—Navajo

We begin our Christmas in the great flowering of summer when time seems unlimited and the Christmas event (and hassle) far, far away.

I always have presents in the house, and at Christmas there must be extra presents for last-minute guests, unexpected guests, cousins of guests, girl friends of guests. So I collect "things," sometimes attached to someone and sometimes to be attached. I begin Christmas shopping at the local island fairs and shops where there are handmade things. Church fairs are gold mines of presents—jewels, antiques, et cetera. I shop as I hunt for shells and stones on the beaches, picking up what calls to me, a random gathering.

There are two methods of Christmas shopping that I use. One is called The Serendipitous Approach, in which the Christmas Presence is felt, not thought about, and is held in one's awareness. Then ideas spring out of nowhere into existence.

Later there will be a moment in autumn when the Christmas List has to be made and, opposite the names, the presents listed, and then the blank spaces filled in and missing presents thought up. And that I call The Cold Plan.

But summer calls for The Serendipitous Approach. A technique I have for thinking up presents comes from the novel by Robert Heinlein, *Stranger in a Strange Land*. It's called "to grok" or "groking." There is no real definition for the word, but when you grok somebody, you sidle up to the person in your imagination and are with him in a knowing kind of way. For purposes of finding appropriate presents for people, it works perfectly, and can be done in traffic jams, while stuck at airports, while waiting in lines and during boring conversations. Sometimes the divine present just pops up, and sometimes it suddenly appears later on. It's like musing, something I remem-

ber doing in childhood. R. G. H. Siu in *Chi, a Neo—Taoist Approach to Life* calls musing a delightful freedom, quite different from "thinking" and "doing." (There is a line of graffiti that reads: "Cervantes said, 'To do is to be.' Descartes said, 'To be is to do.' Sinatra said 'Dooby Dooby Do.' ")

In cooking, the beauties of the day's market present the day's menu; for Christmas, your whereabouts in the summer can present a lot of the presents!

Everyone travels a lot now and treasures can be gathered. In London, Liberty's has wonderful small cotton handkerchiefs, Floris on Jermyn Street the sweetest perfumes and talcs. Last summer in Munich's Glyptothek Museum I was standing in front of a head of Medusa, magnetized by it. I knew why Goethe visited it repeatedly when he lived across the street from the Palazzo Rondanini in Rome where it was housed. He wrote: "This marvelous work of art which belongs to a primeval age of myth expresses a state between life and death," and he called it a "face of exalted beauty." I found myself thinking of Raffaella, so I bought a blown-up photograph of it to frame for her

Medusa

present. Closer to home, in Mrs. Pervear's shop in Northeast Harbor, Maine, I ordered sweaters to be knitted for Nadia and Maria. These and other presents were added to my stash.

So, with the first brown shopping bag stuffed with the knitted dolls, socks, hats, animals, first-edition books retrieved from an old summer-house library, homemade jams, et cetera, the event of Christmas has, in fact, begun.

Still within The Serendipitous Approach are the great mail-order catalogues that arrive in September and October offering all kinds of things: salmon from Norway or the Pacific Northwest, slab bacon from Pennsylvania, Christmas ornaments from the Horchow Collection, a hunter's coat from L. L. Bean and lots more.

I agree with James Beard that food is among the best of presents. One year our neighbor left a gift-wrapped package of headcheese in the mailbox along our road. I give away quart jars of mincemeat with velvet ribbons tied around the necks of the jars, the how-to-do-the-pie included on the label, plus a little bottle of Calvados for drizzling through the top crusts.

Late one summer Nadia and I made rose-hip jelly. There was an afternoon of time on our island, and the rose hips on the bushes of our departed neighbor were in great abundance. Another time we made cranberry sauce from the tiny, wild island berries and jarred it for presents.

One year I wrote an illustrated cookbook for the children, a huge amount of work. I wrote the recipes with colored magic markers in one of those great-looking cloth-covered blank books.

I don't sew but Nadia does, and her monogrammed sheets and pillowcases or linen handkerchiefs are coveted by all recipients. Maria writes Larry a poem each Christmas and this year she gave me a doll that she made. I have named the doll Christina (for Christmas, naturally) and she is beside my bed. She has joints and is wearing a cream satin blouse and a red velvet skirt, and tied to her wrist is a pomander which she drags about with her. Maria says that I give everyone pomanders and that this one is for me.

And so Christmas begins in summer by taking a walk on the beach to gather beautiful things, and sitting on a rock to muse for a while. It can be in a city park, a country garden, wherever

you are. From the gathering, from the musing, grows the momentum which gains force as the holidays approach and can be ridden like the wind, right through Christmas—all twelve days of it.

Toys

On the way to the island each summer, Nadia and Maria were allowed to take one thing. One year the back of our Volkswagen had the following occupants: two little girls, one large poodle and two dolls, Marion and Martin, gifts from the previous Christmas who were the same size as the little girls. "It's one thing," Maria said. I had to agree.

The choice of toys for children can be a way of allowing the essential nature of the child to emerge, encouraging aspects that may be just peeking forth. When the girls were small our house was well stocked with crayons and lots of paper, and beeswax for modeling. All the days were filled with imagina-

tion. Mouse houses were made with cardboard boxes on rainy days, and for sunny days there were the beaches full of shells, tidal pools and caves and the forest of mosses and magical woods where the fairies lived (and still do).

Any child anywhere will live in the flow of life, will display imagination and never know boredom (a blocking of energy) but not if the child is bombed out by an overwhelming array of impressions and sensations; by gadgets that stun mind, body and feeling; by too much television.

I remember a book called *A House of Your Own* which was about finding your house wherever you are: under a table, in a corner, or making a house with two chairs draped with a blanket. Another book, called *Mud Pies and Other Recipes,* includes Mock Mud Puddle Soup, Molded Moss Salad, Tossed Leaves, and so on. A child is like a plant needing sun, water and air. A child needs love and care, good nourishment by way of food and impressions; a child needs not to be manipulated and dulled.

One of my favorite memories is of a kindergarten room with boys and girls sitting together, knitting on big wooden needles. They were knitting scarves of rainbow hues: bands of color of their own choosing. These scarves remained cherished objects for many years; the son of a friend went to battle, when he was a teen-ager, over his coveted scarf. In this school the older boys learned to sew with machines, using the lines of the practice patterns as race courses when the teacher's back was turned; but they were proud of the shirts they made. The girls learned to carve wood, to nail and hammer. We know an opera conductor, a large man whose pastime is needlepointing canvases of his own design. Educators have realized for some years the importance of freeing children from the rigid definitions of what is masculine and what is feminine.

We still give each girl a book for Christmas. Larry gives each of us a small record collection. It is my idea that everyone of any age should have a book and a toy. I like toys that involve movement. I gave Larry a kite one year and last year a bow and arrow, a puppet to Alex, games and puzzles to other friends.

Here are some classics.

Stilts, pogo sticks, riding toys, balls of all kinds, roller skates, ice skates, a sled, a jumping rope, badminton and croquet sets,

a baseball bat and mitt, bow and arrows, a tricycle, a bicycle, kites, a tent.

Theatrical makeup, a simple camera, Lego sets, building blocks, jigsaw puzzles, board games, carpentry tools and tool-box, boy and girl rag dolls, a doll house.

Musical toys, musical instruments: a trumpet, a saxophone, a recorder, a drum, penny whistles, kazoos, wood blocks, a xylophone.

Art supplies: crayons, beeswax (the best modeling material), notebooks of paper, water colors.

And for the Christmas stocking:

Nuts, mandarins, penknives, sweets, water pistols, jacks, marbles, decks of cards, Old Maid card games, hankies with the days of the week on them, small flashlights, small puzzle toys, whistles, wind-up toys and one special thing wrapped up: a ring, a bracelet, a necklace, pretty buttons, fun sox, shoelaces for boots, old coins.

The Summer Workshop

N. R.

Summer has always been the time when my Christmas plans are made. Life is less hectic; things happen more slowly. Lying on your back in the sun is an ideal way to think of presents. Since my childhood, thinking of Christmas has been an incentive to start projects that would otherwise never get off the ground in the drowsiness of summer. When else would I have time to make all the presents I had planned for people, all the decorations for the house? Then there were the Advent calendars I wanted to make for an alarmingly large number of people who deserved them: all to be finished by the first of December! My parents' friend Hugh, who came to visit us in our house in Maine every summer, was my greatest sympathizer, assuring me that it was perfectly fine to start preparing for Christmas in July. I still think of him, grinning as he watched me rush off on foggy days to work in my Summer Workshop.

Potpourri

My hunt for sweet smells to put inside Christmas sachets begins in the summer when I gather balsam, the new bright green growth at the tips of pine boughs. These must be picked judiciously, not too many from one tree, because picking the ends stunts the growth of the branches. Keep your nose alert for good-smelling things growing wild, such as bay or juniper. Fragrant plants often grow in unexpected places. Last summer while waiting for a plane on Nantucket, I found a bush of lavender covered with tiny scented flowers. I filled a handkerchief full of them and stuffed them in sachets the following Christmas. When visiting friends with gardens, poach a few sprigs of herbs such as rosemary, lemon verbena, thyme or rose geranium. Rose petals are the classic potpourri. Let the plants dry well in a cool dark place. Hang the sprigs so air will surround them; lay out the flower petals on newspaper to dry and store them in jars with loosely closed lids. Their fragrance will be preserved until Christmastime.

Dried Flower Pictures

The fields and roadsides of summer provide as many beautiful flowers for drying as do cultivated gardens. In fact, wild flowers are often preferable for flower pictures because they are smaller and more delicate, and easier to flatten. You can collect them as early as spring, when snowdrops, crocuses and lilies of the valley come up. Then grasses start to bloom with tiny pastel-colored flowers. Later come dandelions, daisies, violets, forget-me-nots and, in Maine, wild roses, bunchberry flowers and, later, wild asters—all are preserved in the flower press that my sister brought back to me from England.

A flower press is a wonderfully simple device, easy to carry about, easy to make. Mine has two ⅜-inch-thick pieces of plywood, 11 inches square, with holes drilled in their corners through which 3-inch-long blunt-tipped screws fit. Between the wood pieces lie layers of corrugated cardboard, alternating with double sheets of blotting paper. The flowers are placed between the blotting paper sheets. The corners of the cardboard and the blotting paper inside are cut off diagonally to make room for the four screws, threaded up through the holes of both plywood pieces. The press is then tightened with wing nuts on the screws. At the end of the summer my press is full, the spring flowers at the bottom, the autumn ones on top, ready to be mixed into bouquets for flower pictures.

The assembly of the flower pictures can be done with a pair of tweezers and a transparent glue (such as Duco cement) on various backings. Architect's colored board; a swatch of linen stretched across cardboard, secured with electrical tape on the back; a piece of favorite fancy paper with a faint design, pasted carefully to backing with rubber cement, all can be used.

When I make the picture I am grateful for the few stray grass leaves or tufts of heather that were pressed by mistake along with the flowers, and now I often press a supply of wild greens intentionally. The compositions are sometimes formal, with tiny wisps of straw forming a sort of basket out of which the flowers peek. Or you can make natural bouquets arranged as one finds wild flowers growing. The sketches of field grass by Dürer or Leonardo da Vinci's drawings of plants are inspiring examples of these natural arrangements.

One summer I had the good fortune to sleep in a shepherd's hut on a Swiss mountainside. I was awakened by the pink alpenglow coming in through the holes in the roof and, running outside, I found myself in a paradise of wild flowers. Standing knee-deep in flowers I reached down for a random handful and came up with a perfect collection. The vision of that bouquet has often guided me in making my natural arrangements on paper.

But the luxury of a whole summer in Maine to collect flowers is one I can no longer afford, and so I have found other materials available, even after snowfall, for pictures. From late September on, nature produces her own dried masterpieces in country fields and woods or by city rivers and in parks. Dead weeds and rushes, dried grasses and wild grains, the lovely milkweed pods gone to seed—all have more subtle colors and textures than their living counterparts. And unlike the colors of summer plants, which inevitably fade in the press, these colors are permanent. You can make small delicate pictures with the stems, intricate tufts, and tiny seedpods that are the colors of a Wyeth tempera: sepias, umbers and ochres, faint purples, silver grays.

After the glue has dried, a little spray with transparent artist's fixative keeps the brittle or feathery parts from falling off when the picture is upright.

If the pictures are quite flat, a layer of Saran plastic wrap pulled tight over the flowers and fastened with tape is a simple, easy finish. More permanent shadow framing, necessary for the relief pictures, tends to be costly unless you know how to do it yourself. My recent solution to this problem has been the Lucite 1½-inch-deep box frames now available at any art store. The picture can be pressed between the Lucite and cardboard box that fits inside. Or if the flowers stand out, the picture can be taped to the back of the Lucite minus the cardboard box.

Shells as Presents

Our house in Maine stands on a cliff above the sea and is full of shells. When we were children my sister and I carried back baskets of them daily from our beach walks, as if we had forgotten that for every sea urchin we brought into the house there were already hundreds in bowls on tables, on the bookshelves, in rows along the mantlepiece. But sea urchins are so beautiful and so varied; with or without spines, newly washed-up green or bleached white by a summer in the sun, each was irresistible, more lovely than the last.

Every beach has its own versions of Maine sea urchins: shells so common that after half the summer has gone by, you no longer notice them. Even so, pick up the most ordinary shell when you go collecting for Christmas. A basketful of such shells makes a wonderful present on its own. In December, out of the context of a summer beach, every shell is special and will remind the person you give it to of the sea.

A gift of hand-picked shells arrived one Christmas in the mail from a friend as a nostalgic memento of a magic midwinter afternoon on a New England beach: two large paired clamshells taped together, with a mosaic of fragile shells, shell parts, silver

beachwood and smoothed sea glass hidden inside. An ordinary piece of white coral is very special to me because of the person who brought it back from a dive on a tropic reef, as are the orange snails from Brittany's coast where a best friend spent her childhood. Simple presents like these can grow into a beautiful collection for people on your Christmas list.

Collect for yourself, too. My favorite find is a pure white sand dollar, umblemished except for a single rose-colored barnacle. I considered giving it away and gave it to myself instead.

Shell Pictures

Foraging for the materials for shell pictures is quite different, as the shells must be about the same size and not too bulky. The beaches in Maine retain only the hardiest shells; the more delicate ones are ground to sand in the waves. But every rocky pool uncovered at low tide reveals a rich collection of mussel shells smaller than a fingernail, miniature snails and sea urchins, and occasionally a long snow-white univalve. Other shores are not so harsh and the gathering is easier. Long Island beaches are scattered with pearly yellow or orange bivalves, and small pink-tinged clamshells sprinkle the coves on Nantucket or Martha's Vineyard.

Once collected, washed and dried, the shells are arranged, without glue at first, on a piece of material stretched over heavy cardboard and glued or taped on the back. For a formal composition, the vase for the "flowers" can be a crab shell, a single large mussel, or a "basket" with a weave of sea urchin spines. Small snails, clustered, become Queen Anne's lace; intact bivalves, an upturned tulip.

Some flowers need preassembling, such as many-petaled roses made of clamshells, or daisies made from mussel shells, their white insides facing up. For these, cut small rounds of cardboard and gradually build up the flower from the outer petals inward, gluing each layer with Duco cement and holding it until it dries. For foliage, use seaweed, either the lettuce type or tiny reddish fucus buds.

The pictures must be mounted in frames deep enough to accommodate the shells. They can be professionally mounted in shadow boxes or attached to the back of a less expensive Lucite box frame.

Mirrors and picture frames can be decorated with larger, hardier shells, although these are time-consuming presents to make. Use Epoxy to attach shells to wood or metal frames. A row of mussel shells, blue side out, makes a beautiful frame.

One summer, making shell pictures became popular among our house guests, who nonchalantly dived into my vast collection and, by the end of August, had practically depleted my stores, making dense, intricate compositions full of wild beasts and extraterrestrial plants. Raffaella was the worst. She had an eye for the most perfect shells in my collection; happily, the supply is endless.

2

Into the Autumn

I love the festival of autumn, culminating at the time of our Thanksgiving. It is so beautiful a time of year. The leaves have declared their last salute to life, the harvest is in, there has been Halloween and pumpkins and hobgoblins, and people gather together in thankfulness to great Nature.

Living each moment includes past, present and future, and within the celebration of the harvest there is the recognition of the whole tempo of the year. During the harvest I like to gather and cook the things that will contribute to the event of the winter solstice. Any event must have its origins long before its actualization; so the momentum gathers *sotto voce.*

This is the time to pursue the catalogues (they are available by September), and to order what you want. The supply of things is not limitless, and too often I've been disappointed by waiting too long to order and receiving word that what I want is out of stock. The stores are a nightmare after December first; one can avoid that trauma by gently shopping in the fall. This is an ideal that I propose, knowing that there will be a multitude of odds and ends left to the last-minute rush.

Also, autumn is the time to do Christmas cards. Our friend Gilbert Rose, eighty-five now and not seeing as well as he once did, starts his in the summer. For the last few years he has done churches, inspired by a trip to Mexico, and there was a three-dimensional one this year, complete with church bell. His assembly is complex; he has a line drawing reproduced, and then he works daily all summer and fall coloring the churches and gluing them together. Each one is a little different and I save them each year, as I do Mary Rankin's beautiful botanical illustration cards of holly, poinsettias and the like.

Nadia made our cards for years: angels trumpeting, a silhouette of Madonna and Child, the Three Kings and so on. The finale was the year that Maria's Christmas poems were set to music by Larry, decorated with a cover by Nadia and produced by me. A booklet of Christmas songs, they were sent out as our

Christmas cards. I've been at a loss ever since about how to follow up. I have one smashing idea that I've not negotiated yet; I want to make paper Christmas roses trailing tags that say *Merry Christmas,* box them and send them.

The green light of GO is not yet shining as it does the first of December, but the coming event of Christmas is already in my consciousness, and I find myself musing on the ideas of giving and receiving. They are linked in so many different ways. Emily Post wrote that even the gift of an invitation, accepted or not, imposed an obligation to return the same. The Eskimos believed gifts conferred power to the giver. Their proverb says, "Gifts make slaves as whips make dogs." The wisdom of the American Indians reflected another attitude. Although they did not acknowledge ownership—not of land, which they knew to belong to God, nor of things—they "Indian gave" their favorite things, finding no irrationality in expecting their return by and by. Among the origins of the verb *to give,* according to the *American Heritage Dictionary,* is the Indo-European root *ghabh*—"to give *or* receive." Our own folk saying puts it: "You get what you give."

Cooked Presents

The "cooked Christmas presents" I make are culled from recipes from my mother, from some of the cooking giants of our era and from friends. My mother and James Beard have been mostly responsible for my attitudes toward cooking and the aesthetic appreciation of beautiful food. For food revelers the fall is orgy time, and it's easy to find beautiful produce by the bushelful for canning and for gifts later on. There is a farmer nearby from whom I buy bushel baskets of tomatoes: the Italian pear tomatoes for canning to use in the winter's pasta sauces or in fresh vegetable soup when it's cold, and the regular tomatoes to make "V-8" juice. We have a juice extractor and into it I pile tomatoes, onions, celery, parsley, carrots, peppers—red, green

and hot. The juice is never the same because I use what there is, and the year that I had grown celery and used it with its fresh leaves produced one of the best batches of "V-8." It's more fun to do this with a friend or two because it's a kitchen holocaust. Each batch is tasted, fixed with more this or that and then put into sterile jars and plunged into a water bath according to the book about safe canning procedures available from the government.

Then there are baskets of pears for preserving and chutneys, and in late fall the baskets of quince that are lovely to look at, nice to touch, heaven to smell and hell to peel and chop! A food processor helps to chop them (no machine will peel them). The reward begins in the pot, when they turn pink first and then, gradually, deep burgundy. Their smell while cooking is a feast in itself, and their taste is divine, as is their origin in mythology.

The quince used to be called the golden apple. In ancient times the gods were having a feast and tossed the golden apple on high. The message it contained was "for the fairest" (three little words that finally precipitated the Trojan War). Aphrodite caught the apple and called it a "love apple." Greek women did, and perhaps some still do, give one to their husbands on their wedding nights. It is the love apple that started all the trouble in the Garden of Eden; maybe that's why it's so hard to peel.

I gather jars all during the year for the jellies and chutneys, sometimes even buying something just for the sake of the pot that it's in. I like to make the labels and decorate the jars with ribbons around their necks, or use a bit of sensational material to cover the wax-topped preserves. Maria is a potter, so she makes beautiful pots for her chutneys and jams. Each community has at least one potter who might gladly accept a commission for pots for cooked gifts. A basket filled with jars of home-preserved food, decorated with pine and a piece of mistletoe, must be one of the best Christmas presents there is.

Dee's Greek Quince Sweet

This is traditionally served in a Greek home with a demitasse of Greek coffee, a glass of ice water and a small puddle of the quince sweet on a tiny saucer with a little spoon. And a glass of ouzo!

Late last summer I made fresh island applesauce in Maine and spooned a little quince sweet into the center of each serving as a garnish. It is delicious as a chutney with roast pork, sausage, or whatever.

Peel and dice 3-plus pounds of quince. This is a job; a food processor will help enormously on the dicing. I like James Beard's recommendation for these things—to ask a friend for the day, have lunch, work together and share the results. He remembers his mother's kitchen at such times, as I do my mother's. I love to cook with Nadia and Maria when they are home; a tedious job changes to fun.

However it gets done, the quinces must be peeled and diced and put into a ceramic or stainless-steel pot with an equal amount of sugar and an equal amount of water. Three pounds of diced quince fill about 12 cups, so you will need about 12 cups of water and 12 cups of sugar. Bring this to the boil, and then simmer it over low heat forever, until it turns thick and dark burgundy in color. It takes hours, most of a day. Then add cloves and a cinnamon stick and, if you wish, whole almonds.

"Miss Horti," our neighbor in Maine, poet and provider of hot gingerbread in the afternoons, gave her own childhood edition of Edward Lear's poem with his illustrations to Nadia and Maria just before she died. It is a favorite poem and, being about fowls and mince and quince, appropriate for Christmas. A small edition could be presented with jars of the chutney or mincemeat as a superb present, handwritten, hand-illustrated and handsewn!

The Owl and The Pussycat
by Edward Lear

The Owl and the Pussycat went to sea
  In a beautiful pea-green boat,
They took some honey and plenty of money,
  Wrapped up in a five-pound note.
The Owl looked up to the stars above,
  And sang to a small guitar,
"O lovely Pussy! O Pussy my love,
  What a beautiful Pussy you are,
      You are,
      You are!
  What a beautiful Pussy you are!"

Pussy said to the Owl, "You elegant fowl!
  How charmingly sweet you sing!
O let us be married! Too long we have tarried!
  But what shall we do for a ring?"
They sailed away for a year and a day,
  To the land where the Bong-tree grows,
And there in a wood a Piggy-wig stood,
  With a ring at the end of his nose,
      His nose,
      His nose,
  With a ring at the end of his nose.

"Dear Pig, are you willing to sell for one shilling
  Your ring?" Said the Piggy, "I will."
So they took it away and were married next day
  By the Turkey who lives on the hill.
They dined on mince, and slices of quince,
  Which they ate with a runcible spoon;
And hand in hand, on the edge of the sand,
  They danced by the light of the moon,
      The moon,
      The moon,
  They danced by the light of the moon.

The Owl and the Pussycat's Chutney

In a heavy enamel kettle combine 8 cups of peeled, cored and diced quinces; 3 oranges, thinly sliced and slivered; 2 cups of sugar; 1½ cups each of white vinegar and water; 1 cup each of raisins, golden raisins and brown sugar; ½ cup of minced onion; ¼ cup of mustard seed, lightly toasted; 1 teaspoon of ground ginger; and ½ teaspoon each of ground cloves, cinnamon and minced garlic. Simmer the mixture, covered, for 30 minutes. Continue to simmer the mixture, uncovered, stirring, for 45 minutes. Add ¼ cup of minced preserved ginger, cover and simmer for another 5 minutes.

Transfer the chutney to 8 sterilized ½-pint Mason-type jars and seal the jars with the lids. Makes 2 quarts.

Pear Chutney

Chutneys can be made of endless combinations of fruits and vegetables: marrow (summer squash), apples, plums, pumpkins, tomatoes, rhubarb, runner beans, turnips, beets. The chutney is ready for bottling when it is smooth and thick and all the liquid has evaporated. Then it should be put into clean, warm jars.

Chutneys are traditionally served with meats. We serve slices of cheddar cheese topped with a dab of chutney, accompanied by apples and chilled sherry. A wonderful luncheon omelette is folded around a good chutney with sour cream melting on top.

Peel and core 4 pounds of cooking pears and ½ pound of cooking apples; cut them in quarters or eighths according to the size. Crush 3 cloves of garlic with a little salt. Combine in a bowl the pears, the apples, 1 pound of sliced onions, 12 ounces of chopped seedless raisins, 4 ounces of chopped fresh ginger, the garlic and salt, and the grated rind and juice of 1 lemon.

Tie 4 chili peppers and 4 cloves in a piece of muslin and boil with 1 quart of malt vinegar (or white vinegar) and 12 ounces of brown sugar for 5 minutes. Pour this over the fruit and vegetables and leave to stand overnight. Turn into a pan and boil slowly until thick and without any runniness. This is likely to take about 4 hours. Remove the muslin with the spices. Pour the chutney into warm jars, cover and seal. This will make about 6 pounds.

Maria's Seville Marmalade

Maria's Seville Marmalade is spectacular, and it was equally so the year she used regular oranges. She didn't think so, but everyone else did. The Seville oranges, which are tart and strong, have to be looked for; it usually requires a specialty shop, but perhaps an obliging grocer could obtain them. After devoutly attempting to obtain the ideal I believe in using what there is. Substitution is an art.

Scrub 2 pounds of Seville oranges (or bitter oranges) and 2 lemons, and scald them by dropping them into boiling water. Peel and cut them up coarsely. Remove pith from the rinds and put to one side. Cut the rinds into shreds. Put the oranges and lemons into a pan with all the pith and pits and 1 quart and 3 ounces of water. Bring this to a boil and simmer gently for 1½ hours. In a separate pan put the rind and another quart plus 3 ounces of water. Simmer gently for 2 hours.

Push the fruit mixture through a sieve and add it to the liquid containing the peel. Stir well to mix, and boil off any excess water floating on the surface, or the marmalade will not set. The mixture should be fairly thick. Add 1 rounded tablespoon of treacle (dark molasses) and 6 pounds of sugar. Heat gently, stirring until sugar has dissolved, then boil rapidly until the setting point is reached.

To test if marmalade is set, drop a spoonful onto a cold plate. If the syrup crinkles and ripples when you gently touch and move the surface with your finger, it should be set. This can take from 5 to 20 minutes of rapid boiling.

If, after patient testing, the marmalade refuses to set, don't worry. There is nothing wrong with slightly runny marmalade. We are used to "store-bought" preserves, which are usually made with additives to ensure a stiff consistency. Homemade preserves depend on natural setting properties, which will vary according to the specific fruit used. Let stand for 20 minutes so that the peel is evenly distributed; then pour marmalade into clean warm jars. Cover immediately with a waxed paper disc and seal when cold.

To cover and seal the marmalade, use either paraffin wax and cellophane covers, or make waxed paper circles to place on the surface of the marmalade, and cover the sterilized jars with a cellophane (or plastic wrap) circle held in place by a rubber

band around the neck of the jar. Do not use the original metal covers.

For variety, some of the oranges can be replaced by grapefruit (making up the same weight), which makes a delicious, tangy three-fruit marmalade.

Note: If you are not using Seville oranges, use the rind of one grapefruit and include its weight as part of the 2 pounds of oranges.

Paradise Jelly

Obviously Paradise Jelly takes its name from the paradise of the Garden of Eden. Its color is radiant, its taste paradisiacal.

Remove and discard the blossom ends from 2¼ pounds of quinces, chop the quinces coarsely and put them in a saucepan with water to cover. Put 2 pounds of green apples, coarsely chopped, in another saucepan with water to cover. Put 1 cup picked-over and washed cranberries in another saucepan with water to cover. Bring the liquid in each pan to a boil and simmer the fruits until they are very soft.

Strain each fruit through a sieve lined with dampened cheesecloth into a separate bowl, letting the juice drip into the bowls without squeezing the cloth. Discard the pulp. In a large saucepan combine 2 cups of the apple juice, 1½ cups of the quince juice, and ⅔ cup of the cranberry juice, reserving any remaining juice for another use. Bring the juice to a boil over moderate heat and simmer it, skimming the froth, for 5 minutes. Reduce the heat to low; add 4 cups of sugar and 1 vanilla bean, broken into 3 pieces. Cook the mixture, stirring, washing down any sugar crystals clinging to the sides of the pan with a brush dipped in cold water, and skimming the froth, until the sugar has dissolved.

Increase the heat to moderately high and boil the mixture, skimming the froth but not stirring, until a candy thermometer registers 222° F. Remove and discard the vanilla bean, transfer the jelly to sterilized Mason-type jars and seal the jars with their lids. Makes 2½ pints.

My Father's Favorite Pear Preserves

James Beard

This recipe comes from James Beard, who says he uses Winter Nelis or other firm pears for these preserves. The syrup does turn a delicate pink, as he says, and the pear slices remain firm and translucent. It is wonderful with hot breads.

Prepare a syrup with 4 cups of water and 4 pounds of sugar, and boil it for 10 minutes. Add 4 pounds peeled, sliced, firm pears and cook them until they are translucent and the syrup has cooked down. Fill sterilized jars with the mixture, and add to each jar 1 or 2 cloves, a bit of cinnamon bark and a small piece of fresh ginger. Seal the jars at once.

Special Shopping for Handmade Things

The tradition of handcrafted things is having a great renaissance and will, one hopes, lead to a general wish for excellence . . . Living well with beautiful things is the best revenge against mediocrity. Beautiful handmade things are to be found everywhere. I love the kitchen paraphernalia sent to me from Ohio by a friend there; the best aprons and scrubbing pads made from a heavy mesh gathered into a pouf; practical things of great beauty.

The Etruscans, ancient dwellers of Tuscany, held high standards of beauty for their lives. The walls of their tombs were painted with pictures of people dancing and eating and drinking and loving. (Life is so joyous, they said, that what comes next must be really something; they celebrated death as they celebrated life.) Utensils, pots and pans, chairs, ornaments, clothing —all were "art." To the ancients, art was not something separate from their everyday lives.

The suggestions that follow are from a few people and groups who make beautiful things. I have found these in my wanderings, and others are to be found, if you will search for them.

■ Rochester Folk Art Guild
  R.D. Box 10
  Middlesex, New York 14507

Mrs. L. March, the director of the guild, says: "Christmas glorification is almost our second nature." The "genuine handcrafts" of this group seem to me to be a *genuine* glorification of handmade things. For Christmas there are beautifully and vividly hand-painted wooden ornaments for the tree: angels, camels, hobbyhorses, birds, stars of different shapes and designs. There are elegant original Christmas cards, silk-screened or printed, most on handsome Japanese paper; there are hand-blown glass ornaments in blue, brown, and clear glass with applied silver glass and internal bubble decoration. There are crèches including hand-molded figures and a stable. They also offer straw ornaments, dolls, toys, carol books, and many special one-of-a-kind pieces.

For more information about this guild, write to them and they will respond to you with the same courtesy, care, and attention that they give to their art.

■ Community Playthings
  Rifton, New York 12471
  Phone: (914) 658-3142

This Christian community, with the abiding ideal of a life of brotherly love and justice, is called the Society of Brothers. They publish books about themselves through The Plough Publishing House, and invite visitors, but ask to be written to in advance. Their toys are just beautiful—they make riding toys, blocks, trains, wagons, scooters, cars, all of hard polished wood. Their blocks, used by kindergartens all over the country, are invaluable to a child and can be put to wonderful use by three-year-olds as well as thirteen-year-olds. They never wear out. There is a *real* tricycle, not a piece of plastic junk. There are "exercisers," similar to Junglegyms, strong and light. There is a Pair of Stairs that I would like to have, to make stages and hiding places and for exercise. This is only a partial list. These toys are well made, safe and beautiful. I can't wait for grandchildren—and won't. I'd like the stairs!

■The Herb Cottage
Washington National Cathedral
Mount Saint Alban
Washington, D.C. 20016
Phone: (202) 537-6230

The Herb Cottage sells wonderful things having to do with herbs and seasonings, herb seeds, books about herbs and gardens, cards and stationery and sweet-smelling sachets (you can buy the stuffings for Nadia's embroidered pillows and little sachets there). They also have needlepoint canvases with designs taken from the cathedral's stones. These are illustrated in their brochure.

The pomanders that I love to put about the house in bowls and to keep in closets and to give as yearly presents are available here. Carefully made, decorated with taste, they come bathed in the most beautiful-smelling oils: Lemon Verbena, Jasmine, Lilac, Rose Geranium, Red Rose Potpourri, Potpourri, White Rose, Sandalwood, Pine, Frankincense, Spice, Carnation, Heliotrope, Lavender, Lily of the Valley, Mimosa, Patchouli, Violet and, my source writes, "etc."—whatever the et cetera must include!

In Washington the cathedral is a lovely place to visit, and you can stop by the shop and also the greenhouse where their herbs are grown.

■Ellen Backer
1374 First Avenue
New York, New York 10022

Hand-painted silks can be ordered from Ellen Backer. She will provide silk by the yard or by the finished article, such as pillows, evening bags and, of course, scarves. She makes beautiful caftans . . . treating the body as a moving canvas. I have several; one is ten years old and will never be out of fashion.

One year at Christmas, my friend Gus gave everyone her scarves. I have asked her for ascots for men, and my assortment of her scarves is my wearable art collection.

The technique Ellen employs was brought to France by Russian immigrants in the 1920s. It is commonly called *serti*, which

refers to the fine line of resist that encloses most of the shapes that are then painted in. At times she paints directly onto the silk without the resist, using a technique much like watercolor painting. She says that her designs and patterns and colors come from imagery from the plant and animal world and that she follows the inner movement of the images as though she were dancing. Dancing silk!

■ Sylvia March
 Route 9W
 Palisades, New York 10964

Potter Sylvia March offers a collection of hand-painted ceramic Christmas tree ornaments in a variety of shapes and colors fired to low stoneware temperatures. Most of the designs are traditional: Christmas tree, baby Jesus, angel, star, snowman. Some are more innovative—snowflakes and fiery swirls. If you write to her she will send you information and prices.

She also produces a collection of tiny fairy bowls. They are 1½ inches to 4 inches in diameter; each is hand-painted in tiny patterns and so each is different. These remind me of the classic Winnie the Pooh story when Eeyore finds such pleasure in putting his exploded balloon into the empty honey pot, taking it out, and putting it back and so on and on and on. Children love fairy bowls.

■ Tidepool Gallery
 22762 Pacific Coast Highway
 Malibu, California 90265
 Phone: (213) 456-2551

 3907 West Fiftieth Street
 Edna, Minnesota 55424
 Phone: (612) 926-1351

The Tidepool Galleries are run by sisters-in-law Ruth and Jan Greenberg, artists and beachcombers, who have missionary doctors and Polynesian playboys collecting for them! They say that they will go to all lengths to find a shell, rare or common, if they are sent the name, approximate size, color, and will send

it anywhere in the world. In their brochure they write that they specialize in sea shells, "from the rarest Golden Cowrie to the most common Florida Whelk." They pride themselves on their large collection of select specimens from all over the world. And they have gifts that are inspired by the sea: sculptures, paintings, necklaces of silver or simple sea shells, candles cast from sand.

This year Larry gave sea shells to all, which he had bought in Malibu, and hearts carved of sea shell to Nadia and Maria to wear on chains or bracelets.

■ U.S. Bells
Richard Fisher
Prospect Harbor, Maine 04669
Phone: (207) 963-7184

The ringing of a beautiful bell or gong or a collection of bells and gongs is one of the world's most beautiful sounds. Bells are used in meditation, in churches and temples, and for celebrations, whether they are celebrations of birth or death or the rites of passage in between.

I was delighted to find handcrafted brass bells this summer in Maine at a craft fair. The hanging wind-chime bells are my favorites. The little tea and dinner bells have a lovely sound. There is a catalogue.

Mail-Order Shopping

January and February have always brought the seed and garden catalogues, and I join all the garden enthusiasts who sit by the fire and plan extravagant gardens, whether or not they will have one. (I save the catalogues for decoupage, Valentines, birthday cards, amusement. I've always wanted to decoupage the television as my friend Mary did hers. One year she gave me a decoupaged filing case for Christmas.)

Now there are catalogues year-round that are a boon to busy people, with things from all over the world available to all. It's not the same as shopping—you can't touch and smell and feel —but I can't make my own slab bacon or catch my own salmon and smoke it, and I don't live in Georgia for fresh nuts. Catalogues are addictive and fun, and here are some that I've found. Once your name appears on a few mailing lists, the arrival of catalogues seems to obey some law of galloping geometrical progression: they accumulate.

■ *The Catalogue of American Catalogues*
  by Maria Elena De La Iglesia
  (Random House, New York)

The subtitle is *How to Buy Practically Everything by Mail in America.* It contains everything from antiques to cigars and pipes, to gardening, sports, toys and games and special needs. There are lots of pictures and it provides the catalogue buff an orgy of avarice. I particularly appreciate the section on museums.

There is a *Complete Guide to Worldwide Shopping* as well, the companion to the American one.

■ L. L. Bean Catalogue
Freeport, Maine 04033

I think this year's spring catalogue will be the sixty-eighth (give or take one) catalogue of L. L. Bean. They are certainly part of my childhood, because my father bought all his hunting and fishing gear there. His "Beanboots" were his special pleasure, and this is just how this business started. Mr. Bean came home one day with wet feet and promptly devised a waterproof shoe with rubber bottom and leather top. He sold one hundred pairs, and there it all began. It is still a family business and is certainly on the agenda of everyone who goes even *near* Maine. Fortunately for those who don't, their catalogue is a classic. I want everything in it.

■ Eddie Bauer
Third and Virginia
P.O. Box 3700
Seattle, Washington 98124

When I think of anything to do with goose feathers and down, I think of Eddie Bauer: shirts, jackets, vests, bootees, sox. They have attractive luggage and all kinds of clothes for sports. The quality is always excellent. Some people think their down comforters are the best you can buy.

■ Tiffany and Company
Fifth Avenue and Fifty-seventh Street
New York, New York 10022

Jewelry, watches, silver, china, crystal, clocks, stationery and playing cards; Tiffany has elegant presents for all pocketbooks. The Elsa Peretti pen in my stocking last year writes like a dream and is a silver beauty.

■ Janet Reger
12 New Bond Street
London W1, England

The exotic photographs in this catalogue are worth the trouble of writing so far for, and show some of the most beautiful lingerie I've seen anywhere.

■ Tillotson's Roses
Brown's Valley Road
Watsonville, California 95076

For garden lovers this is a real find. The catalogue is called *Roses of Yesterday and Today.* It is illustrated and executed to perfection, with quotes from Sappho, Lao-Tse, Voltaire, Browning and company. The rose stock it offers is "old-rare-unusual roses" and "selected modern roses."

■ The New York Botanical Garden
Bronx, New York 10458

Here, there are prints, embroideries, sachets, candles, things for the table, cards et cetera. All have a botanical flavor. At Christmas you can order wreaths of dried materials or wreaths made from Maine's finest greenery, herb baskets, centerpieces or a pot of narcissus bulbs, crocus in a Delft pot, a box of tulip bulbs and so on.

■ Grigsby Cactus Gardens
2326 Bella Vista
Vista, California 92083

and

■ Abbey Garden
176 Toro Canyon Road
Carpinteria, California 93013

These are catalogues for Crassula lovers. And to a Crassula lover there is no better present than a Crassula. These plant lovers are a special breed. If you have one of them on your list, write to one of the above for a catalogue.

■ Caswell-Massey Co., Ltd.
575 Lexington Avenue
New York, New York 10022

This is an old-fashioned apothecary. They have all kinds of soaps and creams, shampoos, flower waters, made from cucumbers and lettuce and seaweed as well as roses and such. There

are brushes and combs, nail buffers and emery boards. The catalogue is entertaining and full of goodies.

■ Harrington's
Richmond, Vermont 05477

Smoked hams, Canadian bacon, smoked pheasant, turkey and turkey breast, smoked slab bacon, fresh pork sausage, sausage pie, dried beef, many, many delicious smoked treats.

■ Harry and David
Bear Creek Orchards
Medford, Oregon 97501

Harry and David is one of the most famous fruit sellers in America. They started The Fruit of the Month Club which I think is a great idea. A big box of luscious pears arrived one Christmas Eve, a most welcome present. They make delicious jams and jellies, and gift packages of candies and dried fruits and nuts. And there are pecan pies and cheesecakes!

■ Walnut Acres
Penn's Creek, Pennsylvania 17862

Beneath the address on the cover of the catalogue is this: "Over 30 years of whole food products here on our farms. Without chemicals. Never!" The last *Whole Earth Catalogue* wrote about them, "The best, most reliable source of organic foods in the U.S. Foods like you've never tasted!" They have everything from baking and brewer's yeast to breakfast cereals, cheeses, cosmetics, household items, jams, jellies, honey, juices, oils, seeds, kefir and yogurt cultures and their own flours and grains and beans.

■ Weavers
P.O. Box 525
Fifteenth Avenue and Weavertown Road
Lebanon, Pennsylvania 17042

Passionate lover of Lebanon bologna and pretzels and dried beef and Canadian bacon that I am, Weavers is enough to make

me want to eat the pages of their catalogue. They also have delicious slab bacon and ham.

■Williams-Sonoma
 P.O. Box 3792
 San Francisco, California 94119

They call their publication a catalogue for cooks, and it is. My comment about their last one was that I wanted everything in it, especially their copper *Tarte Tatin* pan, their handmade bay-leaf wreath, their parsley and salad leaf bags to keep the greens crisp. They have a pie pan that I've never seen anywhere but in my own kitchen, an inheritance from my mother. It is of heavy aluminum and has a trough around the inner pan to catch the drippings of fruit and berry pies. All my friends have envied me mine, so it will be a nifty present.

■Trifles
 P.O. Box 44432
 Dallas, Texas 75234

Trifles runs the gamut of "things," as its name implies. Dresses, casual and formal; glasses for beer, drinks; vases; jewelry; Irish-coffee mugs; bed linens; neckties; luggage; things for the kitchen; toys for children. A potpourri.

■The Dover Publications
 Complete Nature Catalogue
 Dover Publications, Inc.
 180 Varick Street
 New York, New York 10014

The catalogue is indeed a complete nature guide. There are books with pictures of and about birds, trees, wild flowers and plants; tips on farming; how to raise insects; floral and needlepoint design; shell art; carving birds; sundials; home dyeing. My favorite is a book called *Boomerangs: How to Make and Throw Them.* Also they offer coloring books of birds, seashore life, herbs, wild flowers, weeds and so on. And bird-song records. They have the home canning guide that I use, put out by the U.S. government.

■ The Horchow Collection
P.O. Box 34257
Dallas, Texas 75234

The holiday catalogue of this famous collection always provides me with gifts. There are all kinds of ornaments for the tree
and decorations for the house. This year there are orchid plants,
brass reindeer from India, gold-plated grape shears from Germany, gorgeous boxes of fudge and chocolate-covered pecans
and Australian glacé apricots, and clothes and jewelry and kites.
For the person who really does indeed have everything, there
is an executive train set: "an authentic re-creation of an old
English train and five freight cars." It comes in an attaché case!

Saint Patricks Cathedral

3

Advent: The Coming of Christmas

*If you go on a spree, then go the whole hog
including the postage.*

—G. I. GURDJIEFF

The festival of Christmas begins with Advent, sometimes described as the twilight which comes before the sunrise of Christmas. The word *advent* is from the Latin and means the coming. For me it is the first chord of the Christmas season. It is a time of anticipation, which some call the sweetest part of any experience. Nature is quiet now, the leaves have fallen and her activity has gone underground.

My activity is not underground but begins with making an Advent wreath in time for the first of the four Sundays of Advent that will culminate in Christmas Day. It is a pine wreath that lies flat on a table in our dining room, and each Sunday we light one candle until all four are lit by the last Sunday before Christmas. Nadia's Advent calendar arrives now, and we begin opening the tiny windows, one numbered window one day at a time.

The making of the wreath more or less coincides with the making of the mincemeat for pies and the baking of James Beard's superb dark fruitcakes. I usually make both the mincemeat and the fruitcakes to be kept a whole year, so that we eat last year's mincemeat and fruitcakes this year. They can be eaten the same year, but must age for at least four weeks.

We have a large earthenware crock into which I put the mincemeat when it is made. This is stored in a cool place and stirred daily for a month, heaven for the stirrer to taste. Then I put the mincemeat in jars and keep it refrigerated. The fruitcakes are well wrapped in cheesecloth and a soft old linen towel, and stored in tins, and from time to time I dribble rum or cognac or even bourbon on them, and top off the jars of mincemeat with the alcohol. This Christmas our pies were made with two-year-old mincemeat, and they were delicious.

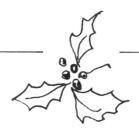

But the mincemeat must be kept cool and the fruitcake tins airtight.

I have experimented with the mincemeat to see if beef is as good as venison and it just isn't. In my mother's house it was no problem to obtain venison because my father shot a deer each season, and we used everything, including the hide for gloves. If there is no hunter in the family, as there is not now in mine, finding the venison can be difficult. There are specialty shops where it is available, but it is reservation-raised and somehow not as good as the wild meat. So I plead with my local butchers for some that they've shot themselves, and if that doesn't work, I drive five hours to a friend's orchard in New Hampshire, where the supply is plentiful. It all depends on whether or not you can or want to go "the whole hog including the postage."

The principle is the same when ordering the turkey. A hand-plucked turkey, highly recommended by James Beard, is superb and altogether different from the machine-plucked ones —not to speak of frozen fowl, which I wouldn't use if at all possible. But if you live in a metropolitan area, as we do, finding a hand-plucked turkey is no easy feat. So I start my search for one at the beginning of Advent. Our turkey is stuffed with oyster stuffing, as was my mother's. Now oysters come in tins already shucked: these must be avoided. There isn't enough juice, and I'm sure the freshness of the taste isn't the same. So I search for a fishmonger who will hand-shuck the oysters for our Christmas Eve Oyster Stew as well as for the stuffing for the turkey.

The trick is to find someone you trust. My wine merchant in New York City is Jack Lang. He will select for me a case of mixed wines when I haven't time for what I call his wine class, a delicious chat about wines, how they're made, why certain Pouilly-Fuissé is called *Long Poil*, for instance. His command of the art also includes invaluable inside information on little-known wines at reasonable prices.

Jack welcomes wine lovers as my florist friend, Gus Pappas, welcomes flower lovers to his shop. There I have learned to make my own wreaths and flower arrangements, and if there is time for us both, we talk about flowers and plants, their origins and lore. A terrarium or a bonsai with instructions for its care is a wonderful present. Most florists will sell ribbons by

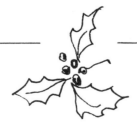

the wheel, or foil for wrappings, or oases for arranging flowers or candles, or all the little ornaments they use at Christmas for wreaths and arrangements. But not at the last minute when they are swamped with work. So I go early for these things and again later when the poinsettias are in, and the pine roping for decorating, and the mistletoe, and holly.

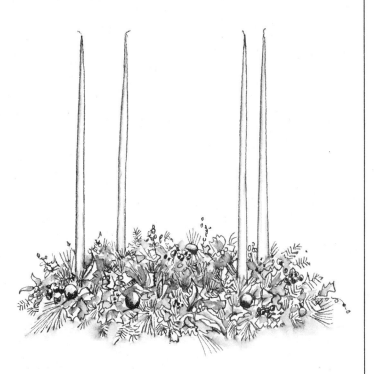

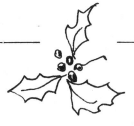

The Christmas Factory

N. R.

When I was five years old, my parents gave me a closet. It was a long walk-in one with shelves and enough room for a red-topped table and a little chair. In my closet I was allowed to cut up paper and not clean up the scraps, draw with crayons and not worry if the line went off the page onto the table, glue whatever to whatever and get glue all over everything. I declared it off bounds to grownups, and in December I turned it into a Christmas factory.

My first factories were small productions, tailored to the size of the Christmas list of people for whom presents were to be made. Since then, my yearly factories have become much more elaborate, with some presents made in multiple for increasing

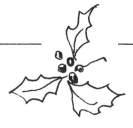

numbers of Christmas guests and friends. My mother now knows to clear her things off my desk in our study before the last week in December, when I come home and turn the room into a bedlam oddly reminiscent of my childhood closet.

Into my factory goes: drawing paper, tracing paper, construction paper, colored and patterned paper; drawing pencils, sets of colored pencils and crayons, nibbed pens, fountain pens and felt-tipped writers; all colors of inks; glues and rubber cement; scraps of material saved over the years (velvets, moiré silks, patterned cottons, felt, lace); embroidery threads and yarns; pillow stuffing; Scotch tape; scissors; gold paint, tempera paint and shellac.

And out come:

Calendars

Every Christmas I make my father a calendar for the coming year. The production of this present is very time-consuming. The theme for my father's calendar presents itself each year, sometimes as early as the summer when I secretly draw island flowers that he likes, wild mushrooms or a patch of moss. The days of each month are written under, beside or within the pictures. One Christmas, after a college semester of botany, I used drawings of plant sections viewed under the microscope as inspiration for color paintings. Seen magnified, the cross section of a flower stem became a wild design; the arches of cells in a monocotyledon leaf became a high vaulted ballroom.

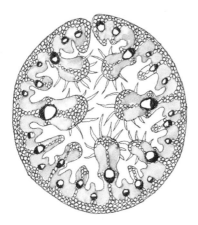
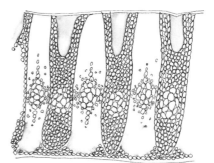

Calendars can also be made with unusual postcards, magazine cutouts or even a collection of quotations nicely written out. They can be wall size, desk size or smaller. One year I made my father a tiny pocket-size calendar, each month illustrated with a staff of music from a composer whose birthday fell in that month.

A calendar is a special present because it is designed with the receiver in mind, and it lasts all year long.

The Christmas Walnut

This is another one-of-a-kind present, usually given to the family. When I was a child, the school I attended celebrated St. Nicholas' Day, December 6, with a visit from St. Nicholas to each class. All day as the classes went on we sat and waited for him, listening for the slow turning of the doorknob. Finally the door opened and in marched a wonderfully tall, white-haired St. Nicholas played, as we later discovered, by the principal, in a very ornate bishop's costume complete with a miter. In his arms he carried a great book from which he read the names of children who deserved a special gift for their behavior in the past year. Everyone was to have a shiny red apple, but only the good children a golden nut. Up jumped Ruprecht, his helper, one of the smaller teachers dressed all in red, who dived into his sack and with great solemnity placed a golden walnut on the desk of each deserving child. The nuts were gorgeous, painted painstakingly with real gold paint so that they gleamed. It was a magic event which I remember when I make the Christmas walnut.

The perfect walnut is stolen from the Christmas nut bowl and carefully pried open. The contents are eaten. The outside is painted with gold in honor of St. Nicholas. (Gold acrylic paint in a tube works well.) Then the two halves of the nut are attached with tiny hinges made of pieces of material glued with Duco cement to the outside of the nut.

Now a miniature scene made with paper cutouts is fitted, trimmed to size and glued into the hollows of the nut. One year I made a Three Kings nut, with a silhouetted procession of the kings fitted in one side, and in the other half, a star against a painted blue background. The year the astronauts circled the

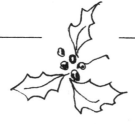

moon on Christmas Eve, the Christmas nut held a little moon with a spaceship circling round it, and in the other half a tiny Earth. To make paper shapes stand out in the hollow of the nut, bend a narrow paper strip at each end. Glue one end to the back of the cutout; let dry and glue the other end to the inside of the nut.

You can use cotton wisps for snow, tiny sticks and leaves of grass for foliage. It is a project for the steady-handed and the patient.

Advent Calendars

Traditionally, on December 1, European children are given Advent calendars to mark the beginning of the Christmas season. These calendars, usually of heavy paper, sometimes made to stand on a table, have twenty-five numbered "windows," areas on the calendar that are pried open to reveal an image within. A traditional Christmas scene such as a church, a crèche, a winter landscape, appears on the front. Beginning on December 1, the child opens one window each day, until December 25 when the most important window is opened. If the calendar pictures a house, the opened windows might reveal a cat, a bowl of fruit, the Christmas stockings, a present, members of the family. A calendar in the shape of a Christmas tree might have each window revealing an ornament.

Begin your own Advent calendar with a piece of heavy paper and sketch your design in pencil: a village scene, a Christmas wreath, a particular street or house, an abstract design. The only subject matter restriction is that your design accommodate the small areas you will need for your "windows." Fill in the calendar with colored pencils, markers or inks. For more elaborate calendars you can use watercolors or glitter or collage materials.

After your design is finished, place your calendar on a piece of cardboard and, using a single-edge razor blade, carefully cut three of the sides of all the windows. If any are irregular in shape, leave enough of the outline to form a hinge. If your paper is very heavy, turn the calendar over and score the hinges by drawing the razor blade lightly across the uncut sides of the windows. Use a ruler so that the scoring will be straight, and take care not to cut through the paper. This process will make opening the windows easy.

Cut a second sheet of paper the same shape as your calendar. This is the sheet on which you will draw the pictures that are revealed when the "windows" are opened. Tape or paper clip the calendar, face up, to the second sheet. Carefully lift each window just far enough to slip a pencil in and mark the outline on the backing so that your pictures will line up with the window openings. (A dotted line will do.)

Now, remove the calendar and draw a little picture within each window outline on the second sheet. Use your imagina-

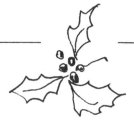

tion. You can draw animals, ornaments, Santa, stars, moons, scenes from inside a house, whatever is appropriate for your scene. You can also cut out little pictures from magazines and paste them in the spaces or you can write messages or tell a story, one line per window.

Spread rubber cement carefully around the "windows" on the back of the calendar. Press the second sheet against it and weight the calendar down with books for several hours so that it will dry flat.

Children love these calendars and so do adults.

Covered Boxes

Little cardboard boxes and canisters saved during the year are great raw material in a Christmas factory. With all the scraps of cloth and bits of pretty paper you have lying around, it is easy to produce a covered box. I made my first when I was young; my allowance would not cover the cost of the box I saw in the window of a fancy antique store on Madison Avenue that I wanted to give my mother, so I made one for her. It had a needlepoint top with an insect stitched on the finest canvas I could find. I stuffed the top to make it soft and decorated the sides of the box with rickrack and velvet ribbon. It was a great success.

Since then boxes have become one of the "stock items" in my factory. Although I make each one a bit different, the basic procedure remains the same. A piece of beautiful fabric, a shell or a picture in a glossy magazine decorates the top of the box. Fabric tops can be attached by sewing them right onto the sides of the box top, through the cardboard. Stuff cotton under the cloth after sewing on three sides. This gives the box a soft, rounded top. Paper decorations and shells can be glued down with Duco cement. Then, to cover up stitches or paper edges, glue velvet ribbon or gold braid around the sides of the box top.

The bottoms of the boxes are covered with a thin material so that the tops will still fit down over them. Cut a piece of material larger than the bottom and sides, and clip away the corners before wrapping the material up and around the box. Secure the material on the inside with glue. This hem will be covered by the box lining, which can be made of felt or chamois. The inside of the box top should also be lined.

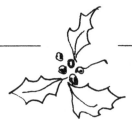

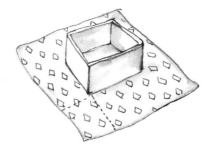

I think it is rather disappointing to open a box, no matter how beautiful, and find nothing inside, so I always put in a sea treasure from the summer, a dried butterfly or just a little folded note written in red or green ink.

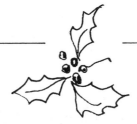

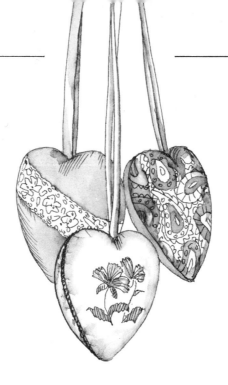

Sachets

Every year I sew sweet-smelling pillows for the ladies on my list, although my father has several of my pine pillows in his drawer as well. One can never have enough of them. They can be tiny, a few inches wide, or large enough to put under your head. My friend Anne, who has Russian ancestry, carries a small, very worn, very soft pillow with her wherever she goes. It still smells of some sweet herb, after all the years she has had it. It is a Russian tradition to lay it under your head before sleep and think of all the people you love.

Our sense of smell has remained relatively unchanged during our evolution. As our brains developed, the nervous center for smell still lay in a primitive part of the organ. It may be for this reason that a certain odor can evoke such vivid memories, even bring back long-forgotten emotions. In the folklore of scent, different smells are associated with special qualities: rosemary stands for remembrance, roses are an expression of love and thyme is the enchanted herb; smelling it enables one to see the fairies.

Making these fragrant pillows is simple. Cut out the two sides (square, round, heart or diamond) from a pretty piece of cloth.

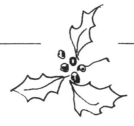

Sew up three edges, right sides together. Turn the pillows right side out and stuff them. Quilt batting makes great stuffing. The little ones I stuff tightly, but the bigger ones I often leave soft, like Anne's old pillow. The good-smelling material can be the lavender or balsam collected in the summer, or potpourri bought in a specialty store. Every December I make a trip to Caswell-Massey in New York for sandalwood, something not available in the wilds of New England. Stuff a pinch of herb or spice in a hollow made in the center of the batting so that it cannot be felt from the outside. Then the fourth side is sewn up and decorations are attached to the outside: golden tassels from a notions store, ribbon binding on the seams or a lace trim. You can make heart-shaped sachets for a clothes closet or to wear. They hang on ribbons or silk cord. A pebble inside helps them hang well.

For added decoration, embroider a flower or someone's initial on one side of the pillow before sewing up the seams. One of my mother's pillows has a pretty lady appliquéd and embroidered on it. Another has a bouquet of flowers stitched in needlepoint as one of the sides. I once made her a basketful of tiny pillows, each with a different smell.

Shoe Mice

These are alternatives to shoe trees. The mice are the shape of the toe of a shoe. They hide in your shoes and are pulled out by their tails. They can be stuffed with sweet smells too.

They are made by cutting out two pieces of cloth from each pattern, sewn up by hand, right sides together, leaving a little space for stuffing. After they are turned right side out, stuffed and sewn up, tails made out of crocheted chains are attached, and eyes, nose and ears are embroidered on.

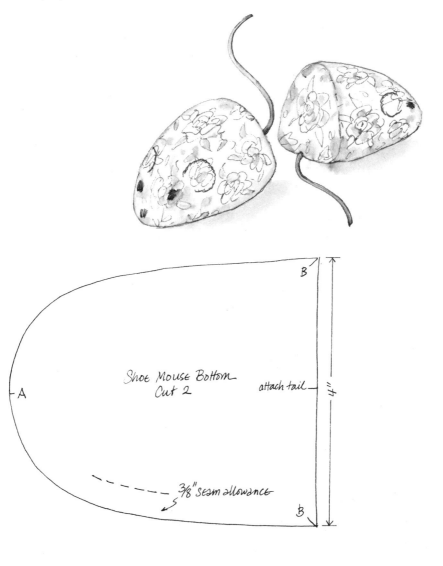

Shoe Mouse Bottom
Cut 2

A

B

attach tail

4"

B

3/8" seam allowance

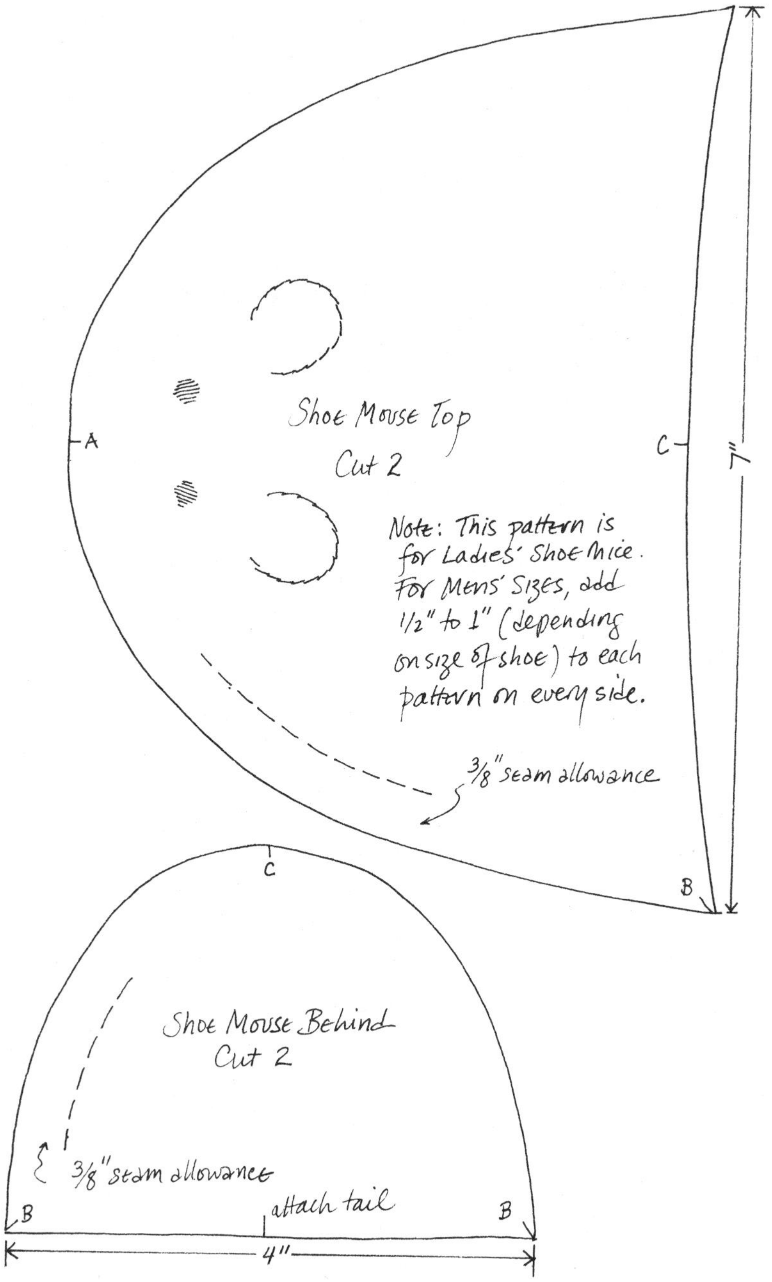

Shoe Mouse Top
Cut 2

Note: This pattern is
for Ladies' Shoe Mice.
For Mens' Sizes, add
1/2" to 1" (depending
on size of shoe) to each
pattern on every side.

A

C

7"

B

3/8" seam allowance

C

Shoe Mouse Behind
Cut 2

3/8" seam allowance

B

B

attach tail

4"

Embroidered Handkerchiefs and
Monogrammed Sheets

One Christmas a family friend gave me a set of embroidery threads that has lasted to this day. It contained every color and shade imaginable. The green section alone was a wonder: gray greens, apple greens, turquoises, olives, kelly greens, viridians. With a set like this it is possible to capture tones and shadows, to create a three-dimensional effect in thread. At one point I had grandiose dreams of making my mother a cape covered with flowers, birds and a deer, her favorite animal. It never materialized, but my enthusiasm for this kind of needlework remains and is unleashed every year in my Christmas Factory, when I produce embroidered handkerchiefs and mono-grammed sheets.

Handkerchiefs require a little embroidery hoop. Design the pattern on paper first, and ink it in. Then trace it onto the handkerchief with a hard sharp pencil and embroider over the pencil marks. (The pencil marks come out in the wash.) The choice of design depends on the person for whom it is made. My grandfather liked to hunt, so his handkerchief had a big ant-lered stag in the corner. My father has two handkerchiefs with a treble and bass clef. I made use of my grand green-thread collection on Gus's handkerchief because he is a florist and green is his favorite color. I also use pure white sometimes, which looks very elegant. The designing of the embroidery is my favorite part of the production. Designs for people occur to me at odd times: while riding the subway, during work, in a museum.

My mother once ordered a set of monogrammed sheets and pillowcases as a Christmas present from me, and now almost every year she gets a new set, with new colors, still done in the same design I made for her years ago. The monogram is done on the hem of the sheet and pillowcase, where there is a double layer of material, so that the stitches don't go through both layers. My color schemes are sometimes brightly contrasting (pink, blue, green), sometimes murky (gray, purple, brown), depending upon which colors my mother fancies that year.

Designing monograms is a visual game: given someone's initials, how can you most gracefully or amusingly arrange them? I recently designed a monogram for Gus with his initials fitted into a leaf shape. My search for unusual lettering leads me to calligraphy books or to old texts with elaborate title pages.

A word on stitches: I primarily use the satin stitch because it gives the illusion of surface. French knots, daisy stitches and line stitches are good for stamens, leaves, stems and outlines. Recently embroidery has enjoyed a rise in popularity and there are wonderful books (I am thinking specifically of those written by Erica Wilson and of one by Mariska Karasz called *Adventure in Stitches*) with fantastic stitches I have not yet tried. Perhaps next year.

Making a Doll—Sinners to Saints

M.R.

Doll making is the invention of characters—bringing people from your imagination to life. Dolls make wonderful presents, for young or old or in-between. They can be realistic or fantastic, elaborate or plain, sophisticated or simple, according to your own ideas and taste. Dolls are not only toys for children; some adults are young at heart, too!

Following is a basic outline for making a doll. Use it as a guide; draw your own pattern and invent all the elaborations.

First, on tracing paper, draw the body the desired size, keeping in mind that it will be narrower when stuffed. Then draw an outline ½ inch outside the figure. This is the actual cutting line which allows room for the seams. Pin the drawing onto a double layer of strong cotton, with the right sides of the material toward each other, facing inward.

Either by hand or machine, stitch along the inner line through both layers of material and the paper. Leave an opening, along the side of the torso, long enough to turn the material inside out and put in the stuffing. Cut the pattern out along the outside line. Then rip off the paper. Make a few small cuts toward the seam, in the neck, armpits and crotch. Then turn the material inside out, pressing out the tight corners with a knitting needle or something similar.

Stuff the doll with any commercial foam or filler, or with rags.

To make joints such as wrists and elbows, stuff the limbs up to the desired joint, then stitch across it. Do not put too much stuffing near the seam, or it will be hard to sew and will make a stiff joint. When the doll is filled evenly without lumps, stitch it closed with small, neat whipstitches.

To make the face, use buttons for eyes, or embroider them as well as the nose and mouth. Draw or paint cheeks, dimples, beauty marks, beards. Yarn can also be used for beards.

For hair, use real hair or yarn. Wrap hair or yarn around a few fingers, sew one end to the head and cut all the loops of the other end. Add bangs, layers or braids; use different colors or decorate hair with ribbons.

Clothes will add character to the dolls. Here is a list of materi-

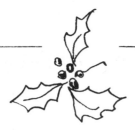

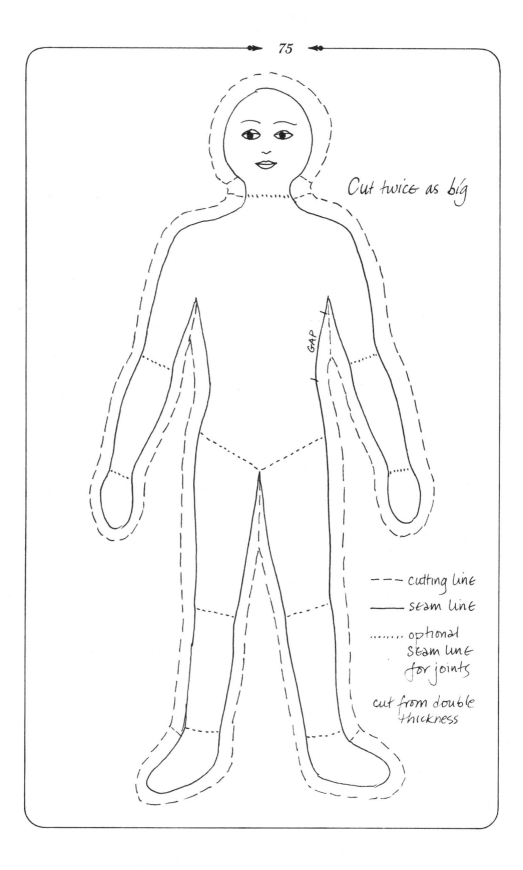

Cut twice as big

GAP

- - - cutting line

——— seam line

.... optional
seam line
for joints

cut from double
thickness

als to use, and add whatever is at hand. A visit to a notions shop for bits and pieces can be very useful.

Scraps of material—leather, felt, cotton, et cetera, lace, buttons (toy buttons for dolls' clothes are available), yarn, threads, ribbons, watercolors, acrylics, makeup, colored pencils.

Sew skirts, tops, trousers, saris, bathing suits. Knit or crochet sweaters, scarves, slippers, or make little felt or leather shoes that slip on. Do not sew the clothes to the doll, as they can never then be washed or changed.

Here are some characters to elaborate on if you are short of ideas:

Girls, boys, fishermen, kings, queens, businessmen, celebrities, gypsies, bums, pirates, athletes, grandparents, a friend, yourself.

Christmas Cooking and Baking

Part of the Bates system for the exercise and health of the eyes is imagery. When Larry was asked by his teacher to imagine a feeling of utmost security, relaxation and absence of stress he was transported back to childhood with his grandmother in the kitchen making noodles. He saw her rolling out the noodles, smelt the dough and was once more in the warmth and ambience of that kitchen. My own memories of my mother's kitchen during holiday and everyday times include the smell of rising bread, of baking cookies, and most of all the beauty, sweetness and gentleness of her presence.

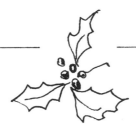

A food processor is a boon to a kitchen, especially at party and holiday times. It shortens the time needed to make mincemeat by easily half because it will chop the meat and the apples, two major time consumers. I think anyone who owns a processor will know when to use it in these recipes. A word of caution when slicing, chopping or grating candied fruits: Citron will get along well in a processor but pineapple, cherries and the softer candied fruits turn to a sugary and useless mush. Lemon and orange peel are all right, too. It's wonderful for nuts. I use it for the batter for the fruitcakes, for pastry, pasta . . . everything but mashed potatoes which do indeed turn to glue, just as the books say.

CHRISTMAS MEATS

This recipe is derived from *Gourmet* and tastes like my mother's did. They say you can use beef instead of the venison, but do so only if venison is just not to be had.

Tipsy Oregon Mincemeat Pie

Boil 3½ pounds venison until tender, and cool it in the cooking water. Put the meat through a food chopper with 1 pound of beef suet, using a fine blade. Blend with 7½ pounds firm green apples, cored but unpeeled and finely chopped (the food processor saves hours here). Make a syrup by heating 1 quart of sweet cider with 4 pounds of sugar. When the sugar is melted, bring the syrup to a boil and add to it the ground mixture.

Again bring to a boil, simmer for 5 minutes and add 1 tablespoon of salt, ½ teaspoon of white pepper, 2 tablespoons each of ground cinnamon and nutmeg and 1 tablespoon each of allspice and mace. Then add 2 tablespoons pitted and chopped olives, 2 pounds each of seeded raisins and currants and ½ pound each of candied citron, orange and lemon peel, coarsely chopped. Add 3 pints of sherry and 1 pint of brandy and stir until well blended.

Turn the mincemeat into covered stone crocks or glass jars. Stir the mélange daily for 3 weeks, or shake the glass jars once

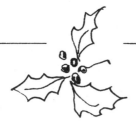

a day for the same time. Store in a cool place and add a little brandy just before baking the pies.

You can use rum instead of brandy, or bourbon, or all three!

Ya Ya's Sausages

Ya Ya is Greek for "Grandma." This Ya Ya is one of the most wonderful women I know. She is old, lively and beautiful, her cooking an inspiration, as is her life.

These sausages can be dried and frozen. Dried, they are a marvelous present; freeze them for long-term keeping. They are always made in big quantities by Ya Ya because they are a lot of time-consuming work, she says, and it is nice to have a good supply.

Dice 20 pounds of lean pork shoulder or butt. This takes a day in itself (but not if you have a food processor). Combine the pork with 3 large diced leeks and cinnamon, cloves and salt to taste. (Remember to cook a teaspoonful to taste the mixture; never eat raw pork.) You can add some orange peel or even oranges to the mixture if you like. This is optional. When it tastes the way you want it to, stuff the mixture into casings. Casings can be bought at Italian pork centers, or you can ask for them at your supermarket. In order to clean the casings thoroughly, Ya Ya turns them inside out, using a pencil, and washes them well. When stuffed, the casings are tied with a thread on each end.

To dry the sausages, hang them on a stick and place them in a draft—such as in the attic—for 3 days. *Or* if you don't have a draft, hang them in a boiler room for 24 hours. After the drying, freeze what will not be eaten or given away soon.

Hella came to our house Christmas with her paté as a present and her contribution to the day. It was delicious.

Hella's Paté

Heat 1 can of beef consommé and stir in ¾ of a package of unflavored gelatin, being careful not to boil it. Add a few drops of sherry or port wine and set aside to cool.

Saute ¾ pound of chicken livers in ¼ pound (1 stick) of sweet butter, and put in a blender with 1 small package of cream

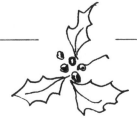

cheese, a pinch of thyme and a pinch of sugar, ¼ cup of cream sherry and 2 tablespoons of Calvados. Add salt and pepper to taste. Pour the paté into a crock or individual molds, and chill until it begins to set. Then spoon the beef consommé mixture gently on top of the paté, to form an aspic. This will keep in the refrigerator for weeks if the aspic seal is unbroken.

Note: This paté is awfully good on sourdough bread with a crackling cold Sancerre wine.

FRUITCAKES

White Fruitcake

James Beard says that their white fruitcake was delicate and difficult to slice but rewarding as to flavor. Sometimes they used almonds in it and sometimes pecans. And one year his mother added slivered candied ginger to the fruit with startling success. The ginger tends to overshadow the other flavors, but he thinks we would find this variation worth trying.

For the fruit: combine ¾ pound of candied citron cut in paper-thin slices, ¼ pound of candied pineapple cut in shreds; ¼ pound of candied cherries—sometimes you can get the white ones, which make the cake more attractive for me—and ½ pound of bleached sultana raisins. Mix the nuts—1 pound of sliced almonds available in tins or at bakery supply shops and ½ pound of blanched almonds or ½ pound of pecans. Sift ½ cup of flour over the fruits and nuts, and blend.

For the cake: cream ¾ pound of butter well, and gradually add 2 cups of sugar. Separate 6 eggs. Beat the yolks rather well and add them to the sugar and butter mixture. Add ¼ cup of sherry and ½ cup of cognac alternately with 3½ cups of sifted flour. When the batter is well blended, fold in the fruit. Beat 6 egg whites till they are stiff and glossy but not dry, and just before they are ready to be added, beat in 1 teaspoon of cream of tartar. Fold this into the fruit and batter mixture lightly but firmly.

Have four small pans or small molds ready. If you can get the small 6-inch bread pans, they are ideal. Line them with buttered paper or with silicon paper, and fill them with the mixture. I usually arrange some whole blanched almonds and a few cherries on the top. Bake at 275° F. for about 2 hours.

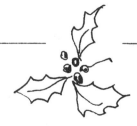

My Mother's Black Fruitcake
(also used for wedding cakes)

James Beard

First preparation: cut into thin shreds ½ pound of citron, ¼ pound of orange peel, and 1 pound of candied pineapple, and halve ½ pound of cherries. Combine these with 1 pound of seeded raisins, ½ pound of sultana raisins, and ½ pound of currents. Add to this mixture a cup of cognac and let it sit, covered, in the refrigerator for 2 days. Toast ½ pound of filberts in a 350° F. oven for 30 minutes. Chop them coarsely or leave them whole as you wish.

On the day you bake the cake, remove the fruit from the refrigerator, sprinkle ½ cup of sifted flour over it and blend the mixture well. Add the nuts and mix again.

Sift 1½ cups of flour and then measure to exactly 1½ cups. Combine the flour with 1 teaspoon of cinnamon, a pinch of ground cloves, ½ teaspoon of mace and a touch of nutmeg. Add ½ teaspoon of baking soda.

Cream together 2 sticks of butter and 2 cups of sugar. Use part brown sugar if you wish. Add 6 slightly beaten eggs, 3 ounces of unsweetened grated chocolate, another ¼ cup of cognac. Blend all this very firmly with the flour, which you should add a little at a time. When it is perfectly blended, pour over the fruit and nut mixture and mix well with your hands.

Line a pan or pans with silicon paper or brown paper. If you use brown paper you will need to butter the pans first. For fruitcake I like to use 9-inch bread pans or one large square pan or two 9-inch spring molds. The cakes should be baked at 275°F. If bread pans are used, only 1½ hours baking time is required. Cakes baked in the square pan or in spring molds take about 2½ to 3½ hours. If you use a very large spring mold, the cake should bake about an hour longer.

Let the fruitcake stand for an hour or more after it comes from the oven.

When it was just warm, Mrs. Beard used to add a bath of cognac and put the cakes in tins to rest till they were ready to be used. She would make five times this recipe every year and often kept the cakes through the year with towels dampened in cognac wrapped around them, and in airtight containers.

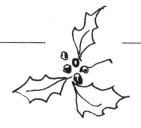

I don't make five times the recipe, but I keep the cakes for next year, and there is no doubt about their superior texture and taste.

Vera's Sacher Torte

Nadia's friend Vera grew up in Prague and this is her version of Sacher Torte from her childhood in Czechoslovakia.

Preheat your oven to 350°F. Butter and flour two 9 x 2½" round cake pans (or you may line them with circles of waxed paper). Heat 6½ ounces of semisweet chocolate, which has been broken or chopped up into chunks, until it melts. Separate 10 eggs, and in a small bowl break up the yolks of 8 of the eggs with a fork. Then beat in the melted chocolate, ¼ pound (1 stick) of sweet butter, melted, and 1 teaspoon of vanilla extract.

Beat the whites of the 10 eggs with a pinch of salt; then add ¾ cup of sugar, 1 tablespoon at a time, and continue to beat until stiff. Mix about ⅓ of the egg whites into the yolk-chocolate mixture; then reverse the process and pour the chocolate over the remaining egg whites. Sprinkle 1 cup of sifted all-purpose flour over the top.

Fold the whites and the chocolate mixture together until perfectly mixed. Pour into the prepared cake pans and bake until puffed and dry and a toothpick stuck in the center of one of the layers comes out clean.

When the cake is cool, spread one layer with ½ cup of apricot jam and put the other layer on top of it; then pour the chocolate glaze evenly over the cake.

Chocolate Glaze   In a small heavy saucepan, combine 3 ounces of unsweetened chocolate, broken or chopped into small chunks, with 1 cup of heavy cream, 1 cup of sugar and 1 teaspoon of corn syrup. Stirring constantly with a wooden spoon, cook on low heat until the chocolate and sugar are melted; then raise the heat to medium and cook without stirring for about 5 minutes, or until a little of the mixture dropped into a glass of cold water forms a soft ball.

In a small mixing bowl beat 1 egg lightly, then stir 3 tablespoons of the chocolate mixture into it. Pour this into the remaining chocolate in the saucepan and stir it briskly. Cook over

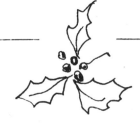

low heat, stirring constantly, for 3 or 4 minutes, or until the glaze coats the spoon heavily. Remove the pan from the heat and add 1 teaspoon of vanilla extract. Cool the glaze to room temperature before pouring over the cake. Use a metal spatula to smooth the glaze once it is poured over the cake and let the cake stand until the glaze stops dripping; then with 2 metal spatulas, transfer the cake to a plate and refrigerate it for 3 hours to harden the glaze. Remove the Sacher Torte from the refrigerator 30 minutes before serving.

Serve with whipped cream.

MY GRANDMOTHER'S CHRISTMAS COOKIES

My grandmother's German Christmas cookies came in tins from Ohio each year. The smell of anise still reminds me of those tins. A lot of them had to age, some were iced, all were delicious.

Lebkuchen

The night before the cookies are to be made, heat 1 pound of strained honey until hot. Stir in enough sifted flour to make a stiff dough and set aside to cool.

In the morning beat 6 eggs together with 1 pound of powdered sugar until light. Using a wooden spoon, work until smooth. Mix ½ teaspoon of baking soda with 2 teaspoons of

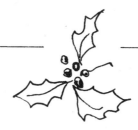

cinnamon, 1 teaspoon of cloves and 1 teaspoon of grated nutmeg and sift with 4 cups of sifted flour. Add the grated rind of 2 lemons, ½ pound of chopped citron and ½ pound of blanched and shredded almonds to the honey-and-flour mixture. Combine this with the eggs-and-sugar and the flour-and-spice mixtures. Stir the dough well and let it stand for 24 hours or more to ripen and mellow.

Knead the dough lightly, adding more flour if necessary, to roll into a sheet about ¼-inch thick. Cut into oblong pieces about 2 inches wide and 3 inches long, or into rounds and hearts if you wish.

Bake the cookies on a buttered sheet in a moderate oven (350°F.) for 15 to 20 minutes, or until very lightly colored.

Frost while still warm with an icing made of powdered sugar mixed to spreading consistency with cream and lemon juice. While the icing is still soft, you may decorate the cookies with chopped nuts or candied fruit.

Schokolade Platzchen

Beat 4 egg whites until very stiff. Carefully fold in ¾ cup of sugar, ⅓ cup of flour and ¼ pound of grated chocolate. Drop by small teaspoonfuls on a well-greased baking sheet and bake until firm in a 300° F. oven. Watch carefully. They practically bake immediately.

Springerle

Beat 14 eggs until light and fluffy. Continue beating, and gradually add 3 pounds of powdered sugar. Combine 4 pounds of sifted flour and 1 teaspoon of baking powder and add it a cup or so at a time, to the sugar and eggs. Roll the dough out lightly about ½-inch thick. Press a well-floured mold firmly into the dough (or use Springerle-embossed rolling pin) to make the designs. Cut the cookies apart into squares and press them gently into 2 ounces of sifted anise seeds.

Set the cookies on paper to dry overnight. Then bake them on a buttered baking sheet in a slow oven (325°F.) for about 15 minutes or until pale yellow. Do not brown. Springerle can be kept for several weeks in tightly sealed jars or tins.

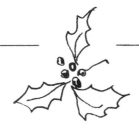

Note: Save the anise seeds remaining on the baking sheets and scatter them over the bottom of the cookie jar or tin. Their flavor will permeate the cookies as they stand.

Butter Cakes

Cream ½ pound of butter until it is light. Gradually add 1 pound of powdered sugar and continue creaming until smoothly blended and fluffy. Beat 4 eggs lightly and add to the butter and sugar. Blend well. Add 2 teaspoons of baking powder to enough flour to make a stiff dough when combined with the above ingredients.

Roll out the dough ½-inch thick and cut out shapes with a cookie cutter. Bake on a buttered sheet in a moderate oven (325°–350°F.) for about 20 minutes.

Frosting Put 3 cups of powdered sugar through a fine sieve. Separate 3 eggs and add a little of the egg whites to the sugar, working it in with a wooden spoon and beating well. Continue adding the egg whites a little at a time, beating after each addition until smooth and creamy. Beat in 1 teaspoon of cinnamon until thoroughly blended. Decorate the tops of the frosted cookies with 1½ cups of slivered almonds or colored sugar.

Butter cakes can be kept for several weeks in tightly sealed jars or tins.

Date Surprises

Beat 2 egg whites until stiff and continue beating while slowly adding 1 cup of powdered sugar. Add 1 cup of chopped dates and 1 cup of chopped nuts. Drop the mixture by teaspoonfuls onto a greased baking sheet and bake 15 to 20 minutes at 325°F.

Coconut Kisses

Beat 4 egg whites until stiff. Continue beating while slowly adding ½ pound of powdered sugar. Add ½ teaspoon of lemon extract and enough shredded coconut so that the mixture can be dropped from a spoon onto a baking sheet. Bake in a slow oven (300°F.) for about 10 minutes.

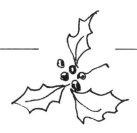

DEBRA'S CHRISTMAS COOKIES

My neighbor Debra sent me these, four of her favorite recipes. The cookbook they originally came from is *Visions of Sugarplums* by Mimi Sheraton, though she has modified them. Debra sent me a note saying, "I always have the help of one of the Christmas spirits who gives me the patience to stuff the sugarplums plump and round, and to make the cookies as small and thin and delicate as they can be," and so she must for these are truly works of love.

Sugarplums

Steam dried figs until they have softened. While they are still warm, cut a cross in the bottom of each fig, open it up with your finger to create a pocket and stuff with a paste of grated dark, semisweet chocolate and ground toasted almonds. Roll in sugar.

Hazelnut Crescents

Cream 1 cup of sweet butter with ⅓ cup of sugar until light and fluffy, and mix in 1 cup of ground unblanched hazelnuts. Add 1 teaspoon of vanilla. Mix 2¼ cups of sifted flour into butter mixture and beat well. Break off pieces of dough and press into crescent shapes about 2 inches long. Bake in a 300°F. oven for about 10 minutes.

Swedish Ginger Snaps

Cream ¾ cup of sweet butter with 1 cup of light-brown sugar until light and fluffy. Mix 2½ tablespoons of golden molasses with 3 tablespoons of boiling water; then add to butter mixture, along with the grated rind of ½ lemon.

Sift 2¾ cups of sifted flour with 1 teaspoon of baking soda, 2 teaspoons of cinnamon, 1 teaspoon of ground cloves, 1 teaspoon of ground cardamom and 1½ teaspoons of ginger, and add to the batter to form a smooth dough. Knead the dough briefly and chill for 1 hour. Roll the dough out paper-thin on a lightly floured board and cut it into shapes with your favorite cookie cutters. Bake at 350°F. for 10 minutes.

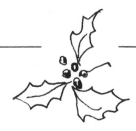

Swedish Spritz

Cream 1 cup of sweet butter with ½ cup of sugar until light and fluffy. Add 1 teaspoon of vanilla and 1 egg and beat well. Add 2½ cups of sifted flour to make a soft workable dough and pack the dough into a cookie press. Press the dough out into rings, strips or any shape you like. Bake at 375°F. for about 10 minutes.

These cookies should not be allowed to brown at all, as they will lose their delicate flavor.

NADIA'S CHRISTMAS COOKIES

Crescents

In a bowl, cream together 10 tablespoons of softened sweet butter (or butter and margarine) and 3 tablespoons of sifted sugar, until the mixture is light and fluffy. Add 1 or 2 egg yolks, depending on the size of the eggs, and the grated rind of ½ lemon and beat the mixture until it is well combined.

Gradually add 2 cups of flour, sifted and mixed with 1 cup of ground walnuts or hazelnuts. Blend these ingredients until they form a ball of dough. Chill the dough in waxed paper for at least 1½ hours.

Divide the dough into quarters, reserving three quarters of the dough, which should be wrapped in waxed paper and chilled. Roll out the remaining dough with a lightly floured rolling pin to form an oblong shape (resembling that of a club or wide stick). From this cut small pieces and shape into crescents. Continue in this manner until all the dough has been used.

Bake the crescents on a lightly greased baking sheet in a 350°–400° F. oven for about 15 minutes. Watch carefully, and when they just begin to turn pale brown, remove them from the oven. Combine confectioners' sugar and vanilla sugar on a plate and roll the hot crescents in the sugar.

Note: Vanilla sugar is made by keeping a vanilla bean in a closed jar of sugar for several weeks. The bean flavors the sugar.

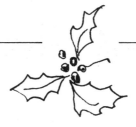

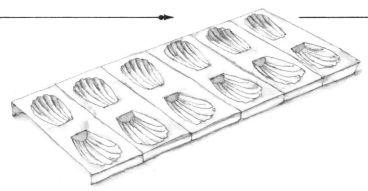

Bear Claws To adapt this recipe to make delicious Bear Claws, make the following additions; the procedure is the same. With the flour, sift in 1 teaspoon of cinnamon, a little ground cloves (depending on taste) and 1 teaspoon of cocoa. After the dough is rolled out, cut off small pieces and press with fingers into a lightly greased bear-claw mold; dough should fill about three quarters of the mold. Do not overfill. Bake the bear claws for about 20 minutes at moderate heat (350°F.).

Linzer Cookies

In a bowl cream together 1½ cups of sweet butter and one cup of sugar until light and fluffy. Add 2 to 3 egg yolks, depending on the size of the eggs, and the grated rind of ½ lemon, and beat the mixture until it is well blended. Gradually add 3 cups of flour and blend the mixture until it forms a dough. Chill the dough in four parts, wrapped in wax paper for at least 1½ hours.

Roll out each part ⅛-inch thick on a floured surface. You need two round cookie cutters, one smaller than the other: 2- or 3-inch diameter for the larger, 1- or 2-inch diameter for the smaller. With the large cutter, cut out rounds. With the small cutter, cut out the centers from half the rounds. (The centers are good baked separately with an almond pressed into each.)

Arrange the rounds and rings on lightly greased baking sheets and chill for one hour. Brush the rings with 1 egg white lightly beaten and, using a spatula, turn each ring onto a plate spread with one cup sliced almonds. Press the rings lightly onto the baking sheets. Bake the rings and rounds for 10 to 15 minutes in a preheated 350° oven until the rounds are just brown at the edges. Cool on the baking sheets for twenty minutes. Spread the rounds lightly with: raspberry, red currant or apricot jam, or marmalade, and cover each round with a ring, pressing gently together. Store the cookies in an airtight container.

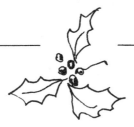

Soupirs aux Amandes

Preheat the oven to 450°F. Measure out ½ cup of almonds with the skins left on; grind them in a food processor, or put them in a blender at high speed for 2 minutes or chop them very fine by hand.

Cream 3 tablespoons of sweet butter (at room temperature) and ½ cup of sugar until light and fluffy. Stir in 2 or 3 egg whites, depending on size of eggs, and blend well. Add 5 tablespoons of unbleached flour, ¾ teaspoon of almond extract, the finely ground almonds and ¼ teaspoon of salt.

Butter a baking sheet and drop the batter onto it by small teaspoonfuls, 2 to 3 inches apart. Lower the oven heat to 400°F. and bake for 5 to 6 minutes, or until the edges turn a light brown.

Remove the cookies immediately with a spatula and let them cool on wire racks or on a cold surface. When they are cold, store them in an airtight container to keep them crisp.

CANDIES

Jeannie's Mother's Date-Nut Bars

Beat 2 eggs until light. Then blend in 1 cup of confectioners' sugar and 1 tablespoon of melted butter or margarine.

Sift together ⅓ cup of sifted flour, ¼ teaspoon of salt and ½ teaspoon of baking powder and add to the above mixture. Stir in 1 cup of dates, chopped; 1 cup of nutmeats, broken up; and 1 teaspoon of vanilla. Bake in a greased pan 12" x 18" x 2" for 25 to 30 minutes at 325°–350°F.

When they have finished baking and are cool, cut them into squares or bars and sprinkle with confectioners' sugar.

Yin-Yang Candies

Jeannie named these "yin-yang" candies because the fudge is dark and the divinity light. The symbol is the Taoist way of showing the reconciliation of opposites and the principle of equilibrium. They say it is the eternal play of the two dolphins, the to and fro, the dance of life.

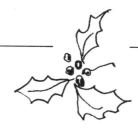

The Fudge In a saucepan, mix together 2 cups of sugar and 2 teaspoons of cocoa. Gradually add 1 cup of milk and stir well over moderate heat. When this is thoroughly mixed and smooth, add 4 tablespoons (½ stick) of butter. Bring to a boil, stirring all the time.

Cook until a little of the fudge, dropped into cold water, holds together in a ball when prodded with your finger. Remove from the stove and add 1 teaspoon of vanilla. Beat until the fudge begins to stiffen. If you wish, stir in ½ cup of nutmeats. Pour onto a buttered platter or into a cake tin to cool. When it is cold, cut the squares for serving. Or catch the fudge just at the right moment and drop it from a spoon onto waxed paper to cool.

The Divinity Butter a medium-size platter and set aside. Beat 2 egg whites until very stiff. In a saucepan, combine 2 cups of sugar, ½ cup of water and 1/2 cup of light corn syrup. Bring this to a boil and cook until the mixture becomes brittle when a little bit is dropped into a cup of cold water.

Pour this mixture over the egg whites and beat until it is stiff. Add 1 teaspoon of vanilla and blend in well. Add ½ cup of nutmeats. Pour onto the buttered platter to cool; cut into squares for serving. Or you may drop it in spoonfuls onto waxed paper to make kisses.

Decorating the House

The evergreen is fresh, green and magically fruiting in midwinter. At the winter solstice, greenery seems to be a charm ensuring the return of vegetation to the land. Bringing greens into the house and decorating with them harks back to Roman and Norse customs that were joyfully embraced by the early Christians. Customs varied as to when the greens must be brought into the house and how long they must stay. Some believed the greens must be burned; others that they must not. Sometimes a sprig was kept to carry luck through the coming year. One story describes holly as springing from the footsteps of Christ as He wanders the earth on Christmas Eve. Other customs proclaim holly in the house an insurance against witchcraft or against becoming an "old maid." Its syrup was said to cure a bad cough.

Mistletoe was a magical plant. Banned from churches, it was essential to the household. Its magic would protect a child from

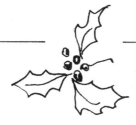

fairies and repel witches, and it was used medicinally for everything from heart disease to snakebite to toothache. The Druids cut mistletoe ceremoniously with a golden sickle, catching it in their robes so that it would not touch the ground, while two white bulls were sacrificed nearby. In England mistletoe symbolized the emasculation of the old king by his successor. Probably our kissing custom grew out of the sexual symbolism. In some places mistletoe was burned after Twelfth Night in case the boys and girls who kissed under it would go on kissing and never marry!

Ivy is dedicated to the wine god, Dionysus. In ancient Greece ivy was called Cissos because, according to the myth, the nymph Cissos danced at a feast before Dionysus with such joy and abandon that she collapsed at his feet. Dionysus was so moved by her performance that he turned her body into the ivy, a plant that graciously and lovingly whirls and twirls and embraces everything.

Our wreath, too, is full of lore. It is a circle, an esoteric symbol of eternity, the snake holding its tail in its mouth. Perhaps we feel its traditions in our souls; and in our genes there is a trace of our past footsteps.

Traditions and rituals are strongest when they remain fluid, when they weave and wind and change. Forcing has no place. Sometimes I decorate the house alone so that it is all ornamented and festive to greet the family as each member arrives. This year I didn't get to the house until Christmas Eve day, and Nadia and I did it while Larry and Maria put tiny Italian lights on the dogwood tree alongside our driveway.

Our house decorations are a medley of objects accumulated through the years of celebrations. We like unpacking them and greeting the old friends that they have become. Some have been given to us as presents, like the two beautiful pinecone wreaths that need regluing each year; some Nadia and Maria have made. There is a peeling silver bell that my mother loved; I tie the mistletoe to it and hang it in the dining room.

And then out comes the Nutcracker to stand beside the big bowl of assorted nuts on the sideboard. There is a lever on his back that opens his mouth for the nut and closes it to crack the shell. He has a fluffy beard and always reminds us of George

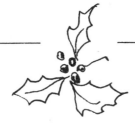

Balanchine's ballet *The Nutcracker.* We first went when Nadia was two, and she burst into tears when the final curtain went down and all the magic was over. So we go back to the magic each year *en famille* as part of our Christmas ritual.

In our garden room there presides a deer head from the stag my father shot the year I was born. For Christmas he gets a crown of tiny fake strawberries, and a green silk ribbon with a bell on either end tied around his neck.

A large picture of Johannes Brahms with a long bushy white beard hangs in the entrance hall of our house. One year Larry made him a red stocking hat with a white brim and a penny taped to the tip to make it fall over. So every year Brahms becomes Santa Claus and greets all the guests as they arrive.

The styrofoam balls that Nadia and Maria once wound around with colored velvet ribbons are hung in a big window at different levels. There are the wreaths that I have made over the years, one of tissue-paper roses and flowers of colored foils that I experimented with at one point. It is a fantasy wreath with a velvet reindeer stuck into its foam base. There is another very delicate wreath of small and lovely artificial fruits and little pinecones and a thin green velvet ribbon, and larger ones, too, with bigger pinecones and artificial fruits that I keep from year to year.

I always buy a big piney wreath with a big red ribbon for the front door and put single small poinsettias in everyone's bedroom and anywhere else that calls out to be flowered. And I like to make a big vase of holly with both the plain and the varie-

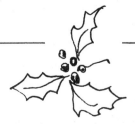

gated kinds. Small clusters of mistletoe tied with a ribbon are put about the house in doorways, and one year we decorated all around the mantel of the fireplace with roses and pine roping. I bought three dozen small roses—red, yellow and pink—and bought an equal number of florist's tubes and put water and a rose into each tube. These were stuck into the roping that had been wound around the fireplace. It is very simple, but time-consuming, and probably too expensive now unless the florist can get some little roses that don't cost the world—but I'll do it again for its beauty and fragrance. The roses lasted well, and when they dried in their tubes, they were lovely in a different way.

I like to float gardenias interspersed with sprigs of holly in a bowl of water. In the middle small tapers are stuck into a metal holder heavy enough to sustain the weight of the tapers. (Lacking a holder, the candles could be anchored in florist's clay stuck to the bottom of the bowl.) But gardenias have to be ordered early. This year they were too expensive, so at Gus's suggestion I used open roses instead and they were beautiful.

There is the three-dimensional paper church that Nadia made one year with its windows to open each day of Advent until the twenty-fifth, when the big double front doors are opened and the figures of the Nativity scene inside revealed, complete with all the animals and an angel hanging from the ceiling.

The decorations look different each year, but these are our basic ingredients. They give a weaving continuity to the years.

The Christmas Tree

The evergreen is a symbol of enduring life. In ancient Rome evergreen trees were decorated with little masks of Bacchus as part of the mid-December Saturnalia festivities. In England the Druids revered the evergreen and celebrated its victory over the darkness of winter. Our present tradition of the Christmas tree is primarily German. In medieval Germany, church plays were performed with the fir tree as the central piece of scenery. It symbolized the Tree of Life in the Garden of Eden and was decorated with apples, ribbons and lighted candles. When the Mystery Plays were suppressed in the fifteenth century the people moved the tree into their homes and honored its symbolic presence with more decorations of nuts and cookies.

In 1605 an Alsatian merchant wrote: "At Christmas they set up fir trees in their parlours at Strasbourg and hang on them roses cut out of many coloured paper, apples, wafers, gold foil and sweets." Martin Luther compared the twinkling candles of the Christmas tree to the starry heavens on the night of Christ's birth.

Choosing the tree has always been an important event in our household. We've had all kinds of trees, with short, medium and long needles. We've cut our own tree when we lived in Ohio, driven to New Hampshire for one cut from our friend's orchard; we've had a magnificent blue spruce which seemed extravagant and ecologically bad, but it was beautiful. I drove through a raging snowstorm one Christmas Eve searching for the ultimate tree. Now I go shopping early, before the crowds and while the supply is ample. This year's tree always steps forth from all those available. I have noted a particular atmosphere at Christmas tree lots. It's quiet, hushed, and suddenly reminds me most incongruously of the atmosphere in a chicken coop!

Recently it has become possible to buy a living Christmas tree. It's an attractive idea, good for country dwellers, but needs

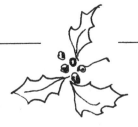

preplanning. A hole must be dug in the garden before the freeze in which to plant the tree, or a sheltered spot must be planned where the tree can wait for the thaw, its root ball heavily mulched with straw. The less time the tree is in the house, the better. Its root ball must be intact and moist when you buy it, and then it must be well wrapped to keep it moist. The spruces (California, Black Hills and Norway) and the Fraser fir lend themselves as candidates for living Christmas trees because they have thick tough needles and can stand the temperature shock of being indoors and then outdoors again.

The living tree can be planted in the garden and with good care will probably survive to be a symbol of everlasting life. After the celebration is over, we take our cut tree into the garden and tie suet onto its branches for the birds.

To Make a Rose

The Persians were so fond of gardens and flowers that craftsmen called *nakhlband* ("makers of artificial flowers" or "festoon makers") reproduced them, using paper, wax, paste and paint.

I share with the Persians, and with most of the inhabitants of the earth, a passionate love of flowers, and at one time made them of many materials: paper, silk, crepe paper, feathers, wax, shells. There are many fantasies to explore, as well as realistic attempts. There is a book called *The Compleat Craftsman* that contains, among lots of other amusing and wonderful things, a very good section on how to make artificial flowers.

This Christmas rose is a fantasy! Use folded white crepe paper and cut out the petals a number at a time. Buy Dr. Martin's Radiant Dyes in whatever colors you like. They come in little eyedropper bottles. Put a few drops into a plastic container with approximately one cup of water. I dip the petals first into one color, then into another, and let them run together as they will, dyeing the small end first and then the large end, or vice versa. These dipped petals are then put down to dry on large sheets of the crepe paper (these sheets become wrapping paper, resplendent with their many colors from the drying petals). When the petals are dry, push a "belly" into each one with your thumbs and, also with your thumbs, ruffle the edges. Now make the center of the flower by wadding up some crepe paper scraps or a piece of cotton into a ball. Stretch a smooth piece of crepe paper over the ball. (You can dye some squares for this in the color pots when you do the petals.) Secure the ball with a thin florist's wire, drawing the paper together at the bottom. For stamens, I use the wildest things I can find at the florist's or floral supply house; little dyed pink pearls, rhinestonelike bits of glass on wires, or little feathers, or tiny dried flowers. You can also use ribbon loops or strings of paper ribbon that you curl with scissors.

Whatever you use, gather the stamens around the center and wire them at the bottom of the ball. Now start to put the petals around the ball, gathering them and arranging them as you like. You can use as many petals as you want; I use a lot to make a fluffy flower. Wire them in place as you go round and round the center. When there are enough to please your eye, twist the ends of the wires around each other, drawing them away from the flower to make a stem. To make the calyx that underlies the petals, cut it out, using the pattern, and wrap it around the stem, letting its points droop as they will; wire it in place, twisting this wire around the stem. Wrap the stem with green florist's tape, twisting the tape well up around the calyx.

This is the flower. You can make buds and leaves and wire them with the flower onto a long green wire "stem" from the

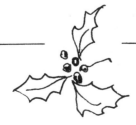

florist or craft shop. One year I made a dozen of these into "long-stemmed roses" for a present and put them into a big florist's box with a bottle of champagne nestled among them.

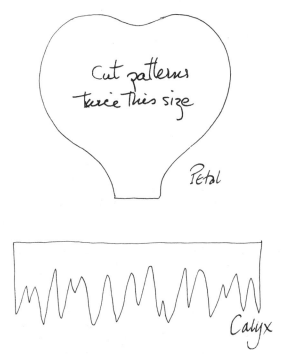

These roses can be hung on the tree; some people use only paper roses on their trees. I use them in my fantasy wreaths as well as foil and feather flowers.

To Make a Wreath

There are various ways to make a wreath. You need a frame, so untwist a hanger and bend it into a circle, twisting the ends together. This hoop can also be made of a bent stripped willow switch, California privet or any pliable shrub. If you want a sturdier frame, twist on a second switch. I used to gather ground pine in the Pennsylvania woods and make our wreath of that, but the ground pine around our house is precious so I buy roping at the florist, or I go through the garden with a basket and clippers gathering snippets of pine, rhododendron,

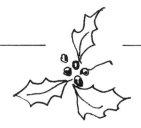

laurel, ivy, sprigs of berries from the wild rose bushes, dried things, whatever I can find. We are great lovers of the winter garden and I take only what it can spare.

Brush the pines and their stems with shellac to keep them from shriveling. I keep a supply of florist's wires in different weights, and use them to wire together small clumps of the pine or dried things, berries, fruits, then wire the clusters onto the hoop. If you use roping, wind it round and round the hoop, securing it from time to time with the wires. Green string or thread can also be used. You can buy styrofoam hoops; for those I use the florist's picks (with wire attached), wire the clumps of things to the pick and stick it into the styrofoam hoop.

For an Advent wreath it is much easier to buy a styrofoam base made to hold candles, and insert the candles. But for the wreath for the door, a hoop seems to give the wreath a grace that it doesn't have with the styrofoam base.

Our friend Mary crisscrosses ribbon in old-fashioned style all around her wreath. There are all kinds of choices for the ribbons: plaid ones, velvet ones, a single ribbon or many ribbons.

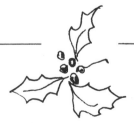

Wrapping Christmas Presents

There are beautiful wrapping papers sold by the sheet, but they can be expensive and there are some interesting alternatives. Colored tissue paper is available and sometimes wallpaper sample books can be had from wallpaper shops; ones that are out of date for them and which they will give to you. These make beautiful wrapping papers. My favorite paper is the white crepe paper on which I spread out my paper rose petals to dry. Their dyes "bleed" onto the white crepe paper and produce a wonderful tie-dyed-like random coloring of many hues. I use this paper for birthdays, Valentine's Day . . . anything.

I buy rolls of satin and velvet ribbons from Gus and also any little artificial fruits, pinecones sprayed with glitter, et cetera. But I use paper ribbons too.

The Japanese make wrapping an art. And so do my friends Alfie and Mary. They save ribbons for years. (I use a ruby antique ribbon from one of their presents as a tie around the waist of a black lace dress.) Their presents are sealed with invisible rubber cement and tied simply with a beautiful satin ribbon or a special piece of string. Or whatever. I tie presents with marlin, a light, two-stranded string that I buy in the boat supply yard; it smells of tar, and on the right paper it is attractive and unusual. This year paper was so expensive I wrapped some presents in brown paper bags tied with big ribbons. The point is that anything goes, including a big package wrapped in white tissue paper tied with a mad "ribbon" drawn on with magic markers in many colors.

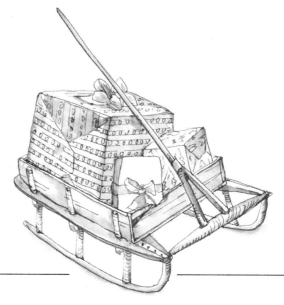

the
CELEBRATION

The Season of the Holy Nights

4

Christmas Eve

For a few days, once a year,
the atrophied souls of the grown-ups
are filled again with that spirit
which inspires the wisdom of fools and children.

—MICHAEL HARRISON

Our celebration begins on the afternoon of Christmas Eve at teatime. The turkey has been called for at the butcher's and the oysters at the fish market, the bread for the stuffing has been cut into small cubes and is drying on trays, the cranberry sauce is made, the *Christollen* started and the tree is in the house, warming up. It is time to find its perfect side, guy it in place, pour some dark rum into the Lapsang Souchong tea we are drinking and begin to put the lights on the tree.

One year at about this time of day a wonderful actor friend arrived in his sleigh drawn by two of his beautiful horses to deliver his Christmas card—a large (at least two feet high) gingerbread man with Merry Christmas and the family's names written in white icing. The sleigh came into our driveway, its bells ringing, with our very merry friend at the reins getting merrier all the time from wassailing at each house.

Arriving house guests and the general flurry of things have determined our Christmas Eve menu: oyster stew, smoked salmon and fruit soup. We have friends who send us a whole smoked salmon, beautifully wrapped. This year, Zabar's in New York City sold attractively packaged ones to send as gifts or to have for yourselves, and salmon is included in many of the food catalogues. This rather spare menu suits us well because the next day is feast day and all the excitement and things to do don't seem to lead to huge appetites. The free buffet style of serving is right for guests wandering in at various times, which they always do.

Putting Lights on the Tree

L. R.

I had the good fortune to be trained in the art of putting lights on a Christmas tree by a master, my father-in-law, whom for many Christmases I served as apprentice-assistant.

In fact, the principle is a very simple one. The beauty of the tree is much enhanced by a sense of its depth. So, instead of merely draping a string of lights along the surface, which does no more than follow its outer shape, you start instead from the tree's core.

Over the years we've somehow accumulated many strings of lights. One of the yearly Christmas annoyances is the string that stopped functioning last Christmas and which has languished all year in the basement, untended to, in a sturdy carton, clearly and optimistically labeled by my mechanically untalented hand in large magic-marker legend: CHRISTMAS LIGHTS TO BE RE-

PAIRED. But now, of course, it is December 24, so dash out to the hardware store for more.

Christmas light bulbs seem to come generally in three sizes: fairly large ones (the biggest ones are actually outdoor lights), the standard medium-size bulbs and the tiny, jewellike "Italian" lights, which are now made in the United States and are readily available.

Once the tree is guyed and standing solidly in place, take a string of the largest, brightest bulbs you have and begin threading them along and around the trunk of the tree, attaching them to the thickest branches as close to the trunk as possible. (Your face will surely be tickled and possibly scratched at this stage, especially if the tree has long needles, but the eventual effect is really worth it.) You may find it easiest to start at the top of the tree and spiral downwards, leaving the end of the string with the electric plug at the bottom where it will be nearest to the wall outlet, or to plug into the next string of lights. The size and brightness of these large bulbs will make their light penetrate the thickness of the foliage and illuminate it.

You may also find it useful to have a helper to hold the other end of the string, to keep the bulbs from clanking together or falling on the floor—they break easily—and also to sympathize with your occasional outbursts of exasperation and grunts of frustration, or just generally to admire the results and to appreciate how hard you are working!

The medium-size bulbs are next. Attach them to branches farther from the center. Finally, the tiny ones (which can usually be made to wink on and off if you like; Maria does, I don't) can be threaded along the outer surface of the tree. Of course, your eye and your taste must be the guide to the number of lights you use and the density of clusters, their symmetry and the balance of color.

In any case, the effect is truly three-dimensional. We always pause a moment, before the ornaments go on, to admire it. The tree is already almost beautiful enough. It glitters but is also suffused with an inner glow, its depths bathed in a subtle radiance. Even a very large, dense tree will appear lighter than air, almost as though it could float up through the ceiling. Last year's tree, a lovely, fat and roundish one, reminded us curiously of the planet Jupiter: gigantic, luminous, ethereal.

Trimming the Tree

After dinner we play music and trim the tree. It's nice to have the ornaments unwrapped and in baskets. I love Christmas tree ornaments and I still have some from my childhood trees, by now faded and chipped and so precious. Packing and unpacking the ornaments is a wonderful trip through my life from child-hood to now. There is the woolen yarn doll, the felt Christmas tree decorated with sequins, the blue duck with a button for an eye; each tells its story. There are the cardboard animals that Nadia and my mother cut out the third year of Nadia's life and the last of my mother's; there are the tin Mexican ornaments that were a present from the year we spent Christmas in a small chalet high in the Alps, put candles on our tree and strung popcorn and cranberries for ornaments.

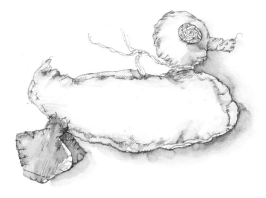

This year a friend sent us a tiny box of German ornaments from Munich. We tie a beautiful French doll on the top of the tree, and under the tree we put our special dolls: some little china ones of mine and one that Maria made seated on my childhood wicker furniture. There is also a village of houses with Santa and his sleigh and reindeer driving through. We sip

mulled wine and sing carols and admire the miracle when it's finished. It's always a hushed time and each year we say it's the best tree we've ever had. Then everyone digs out his presents from closets and hiding places and puts them under the tree and the miracle is complete.

The stockings are still hung by the chimney with care by Nadia and Maria; *The Night Before Christmas* is still read at bedtime, and each picture of the rosy-faced St. Nicholas who puts his finger alongside his nose to negotiate the chimney is looked at by all. We have the book that was mine, old and a bit tattered. Santa Claus's presents to the children don't get put under the tree. Larry and I do that when the children are in bed. Then we drink the champagne and eat some of the cookies meant for us Santas. (A friend once made footprints of Santa's boots and the reindeer's hooves out in the fresh snow!)

And then we go to bed so that Santa can land on our roof and our heads can be filled with visions of sugarplums.

Menu
Christmas Eve

Oyster Stew
Smoked Salmon
Pumpernickel Bread

Fruit Soup

Champagne

Trimming the Tree~

Mulled Wine
Cookies

Mil's Oyster Stew

Mil's Oyster Stew is better if it stands overnight, but in view of the whole choreography at this festival time, the oysters have to be picked up Christmas Eve morning for both the stew and the stuffing, so I try to make the stew as soon as the oysters arrive in the morning and let it mellow all day. When reheating, do it slowly, attentively, stirring often. It mustn't curdle.

Put 1 pint of fresh oysters and their liquid in a saucepan over low heat; cook only until the edges of the oysters begin to curl.

Pour 1 quart of half-and-half in another pot and heat only until there is the slightest indication of bubbles around the side. Turn off the heat.

Empty the oysters and their liquor into the hot cream. Add 1 tablespoon of butter and 1 teaspoon of salt. Sprinkle with freshly ground pepper.

Heat the stew a little more if it is to be served right away; however, this is best when made the day before and refrigerated until ready to be used.

Attention! Attention! Under no circumstances do you add the salt until the oysters and cream have been combined or the stew will curdle. Do not let the cream and oysters boil or it will curdle!

Serve with Exton crackers or other hard round crackers to break into the soup.

Jeannie's Grandmother's Fruit Soup

Jeannie first brought us this cold soup many years ago on Christmas Eve. We love it and have incorporated it into our tradition. Jeannie's grandmother lived in Ohio and her recipes always reflect her European origins. Melded with other heritages, dishes like these are an example of our really wonderful American cuisine.

Make this soup at the same time the oyster stew is made to give it time to chill.

In a heavy-bottomed four-quart saucepan, combine 6 cups of water, 1½ cups of prunes, 1½ sticks of cinnamon, 1 small lemon, sliced paper thin, and a pinch of salt.

Bring this to a boil and let it cook gently for a couple of minutes. Then add 1 cup of golden raisins, 1 cup of seedless black raisins and 1 cup of currants. Stir very gently to combine the fruits and let it cook for a few more minutes over low heat.

Stir in 2 tablespoons of minute tapioca and simmer for 5 to 6 minutes, stirring from time to time. During the last 2 or 3 minutes of the cooking time add sugar to taste—about 2 tablespoons if you like it on the tart side. Chill.

Mulled Wine

Put a good, decent red wine into an enameled or stainless-steel pot and add an orange stuck with cloves. I like to make a design of the cloves on the orange. Add a few pieces of cinnamon stick and a little sugar if you wish; I do not. Heat this until steaming hot, but not to the boil, and ladle it into mugs with a twist of lemon. I sometimes put into each mug a cinnamon stick that is long enough to be a stirrer.

Or you can pour the wine and spices and oranges into a punch bowl, and the guests can serve themselves. Also some brandy can be floated on top of the hot wine and flamed just before serving. Be sure the brandy is slightly warmed or it may not ignite.

The Night Before Christmas
by Clement Clarke Moore

ORIGINALLY ENTITLED A VISIT FROM ST. NICHOLAS

'Twas the night before Christmas, when all through the house
Not a creature was stirring, not even a mouse;
The stockings were hung by the chimney with care,
In hopes that St. Nicholas soon would be there;
The children were nestled all snug in their beds,
While visions of sugar-plums danced in their heads;
And mamma in her kerchief, and I in my cap,
Had just settled our brains for a long winter's nap,
When out on the lawn there arose such a clatter,
I sprang from my bed to see what was the matter.

Away to the window I flew like a flash,
Tore open the shutters and threw up the sash.
The moon, on the breast of the new-fallen snow,
Gave a lustre of midday to objects below;
When what to my wondering eyes should appear
But a miniature sleigh and eight tiny reindeer,
With a little old driver, so lively and quick,
I knew in a moment it must be St. Nick.
More rapid than eagles his coursers they came,
And he whistled, and shouted, and called them by name:
"Now, Dasher! now, Dancer! now, Prancer! now, Vixen!
On, Comet! on, Cupid! on, Donder and Blitzen!—
To the top of the porch, to the top of the wall!
Now dash away, dash away, dash away all!"

As dry leaves that before the wild hurricane fly,
When they meet with an obstacle, mount to the sky,
So up to the house-top the coursers they flew,
With the sleigh full of toys, and St. Nicholas, too.
And then in a twinkling I heard on the roof
The prancing and pawing of each little hoof.

As I drew in my head, and was turning around,
Down the chimney St. Nicholas came with a bound.
He was dressed all in fur from his head to his foot,
And his clothes were all tarnished with ashes and soot;
A bundle of toys he had flung on his back,
And he looked like a peddler just opening his pack.
His eyes how they twinkled! his dimples how merry!
His cheeks were like roses, his nose like a cherry.
His droll little mouth was drawn up like a bow,
And the beard on his chin was as white as the snow.

The stump of a pipe he held tight in his teeth,
And the smoke, it encircled his head like a wreath.
He had a broad face, and a round little belly
That shook, when he laughed, like a bowl full of jelly.
He was chubby and plump—a right jolly old elf—
And I laughed when I saw him, in spite of myself.

A wink of his eye, and a twist of his head,
Soon gave me to know I had nothing to dread.

He spake not a word, but went straight to his work,
And filled all the stockings; then turned with a jerk,
And laying his finger aside of his nose,
And giving a nod, up the chimney he rose.
He sprang to his sleigh, to his team gave a whistle,
And away they all flew like the down of a thistle;
But I heard him exclaim, ere he drove out of sight,
"Happy Christmas to all, and to all a good-night!"

5

Christmas Day

Christmas morning begins with a pot of coffee and a pot of tea to accommodate both tastes. Then the stockings are unpacked. They always contain oranges and some nuts among the presents. My great-grandparents brought my mother and her sisters and brothers an orange every Christmas. They arrived in their horse-drawn sleigh with an orange for each child. It was a great treat in that time before coast-to-coast shipment of produce.

There is a legend about the oranges traditionally put into the toes of Christmas stockings. Saint Nicholas, who first appeared in the fourth century as the Bishop of Myra, gave his possessions secretly to those in need and became known as "the giver of gifts from unknown sources." His popularity spread throughout the world and he became the patron saint of many countries, and specifically the patron saint of children, maidens, merchants and ships. In one legend Saint Nicholas wanted to give some dowry money to two poor maiden sisters. In order to maintain secrecy, he tossed bags of gold down the sisters' chimney. Their stockings were hanging by the chimney to dry and the gold fell into the stockings. Today's stockings hung by the chimney with care contain shiny golden oranges to commemorate this legend.

Then our whole cast moves to the room of the tree and we begin the opening of the presents. There is an art to opening presents. We like to be formal, opening packages one by one so that the present with its wrapping is admired and enjoyed by all. Some openers wildly tear apart their gifts in a mad desire to get to the contents, and others meticulously and, to some, maddeningly, remove ribbons and wrappings bit by bit, cherishing each moment. Both types are included in the *art*. It is a question of individual nature and tempo. What is *not* acceptable is someone who loses himself and engages others in an intellectual conversation while mindlessly opening the package. (Like eating a meal without tasting the food.)

It is an event of giving and receiving. When the kaleidoscope turns, the roles change; the giver receives and vice versa. The ribbons get tied around lampshades or the dog's neck; and the little cards that are often handmade or have been carefully chosen, must not be missed.

Somewhere in all this, which takes several hours, and after enough coffee and tea have been had by all, Larry produces Gin Alexanders, the original Alexander, he claims. They are delicious, creamy, not sweet, not too strong, and seem perfect at this moment.

Next is Christmas Breakfast, and the arrival of the first guests of the day, the breakfast guests, William and Debra. She brings cookies she's baked; he brings books he's read and wants us to read. The menu is melon and prosciutto, *Christollen,* assorted cheeses. This is a quiet time, after all the presents and before the next event of the day, with good conversation and more coffee. For me, it is a restful hiatus before the making of the stuffing, stuffing and trussing the turkey and putting it into the oven, getting the crudités ready, peeling the potatoes and putting them into cool water until cooking time, and checking that Larry remembers to chill the dinner wine and put the champagne in the snow to cool. Champagne must be well chilled. The ice bucket is the way to chill it, or bury it in snow or sink it in an icy stream. The refrigerator is a poor substitute for any of these ways.

Now the breakfast guests go on their way, and the dinner guests start to arrive.

There are many people, music, more presents exchanged; some paté from Barbara and Hella this year; a pile of records for Larry from Arnold, lovingly scrounged up at the last minute from his collection; ruby-red napkins that Mary made, all rolled up in a beautiful old basket. Often friends haven't seen one another for a year; some live in far places, and this is reunion time, an important part of the festival. There is much to say, all the new Christmas-present books to browse in, and we are ready for vodka and caviar with dark Russian bread.

The bread is very, very thinly sliced, spread with just a little sweet butter, and a squeeze of lemon on top of the caviar. The price of Beluga caviar went altogether out of bounds this year,

so I bought fresh red caviar and it was delicious. Put the vodka in its block of ice on a big, beautiful tray. I put holly and ivy on the tray and we drink the vodka from tiny shot glasses that belonged to my mother-in-law. This is served in the living room on the coffee table, with tiny napkins. I slice as much bread as I have time and patience to do and put the remaining bread on a board with a good knife.

This is the nature of our Christmas: everyone is involved, as current jargon puts it, and therefore I survive. The table is set by Nadia and Maria, who know that the silverware must be straight and not too close to the edge of the table. One of them arranges the big plate of crudités, and Gus carves beautifully. (One year at Easter he carved a huge platter of duck, stole Easter lilies from a big lily plant he'd given me and placed the flowers among the pieces of duck!) Place cards are made by Larry, written in his elegant calligraphy.

By now I am busy in the kitchen. All I can say is that somehow it gets done and somewhere in it all we make a toast to ourselves with ice-cold champagne. Gus and I get the turkey out of the pan and onto the platter (quite a feat). At that moment I put the mincemeat pies in the oven to warm while we are eating. Maria made the gravy and the creamed leeks this year, guests mashed the potatoes, and Larry is always the *sommelier.* Everybody always argues about whether to serve red or white wine with turkey. Larry serves both.

Everyone is seated and the blessing is said, and Gus and I serve the plates and it is always the best ever. Dinner is long, full and filling. Our table is huge, and with all of us gathered round it is the climax of the celebration. When the moment is right, the plates are cleared by a few of us, my mother's marvelous pie forks and my mother-in-law's beautiful plates appear, and the mincemeat pie is served with coffee and cognac. There are tumblers of Vichy water to ease the feeling of being stuffed. And so the dinner ends.

The rest is an improvisation. Sometimes we pass around Xerox copies of handwritten lyrics to our favorite Christmas carols and sing. Maria wrote them out a few years ago so that everyone could sing all the verses. This year we danced. We play with our presents, talk and one year of a big snow we all

got warmly dressed, went out into the night and had a huge and hilarious snowball battle. The only mishap was suffered by the dog who was ill from eating too much snow! That night we had hot chocolate before bed. The last event of the day is to listen to our recording of Dylan Thomas reading *A Child's Christmas in Wales.*

It is a day of delight. Family, friends and the traditions we love.

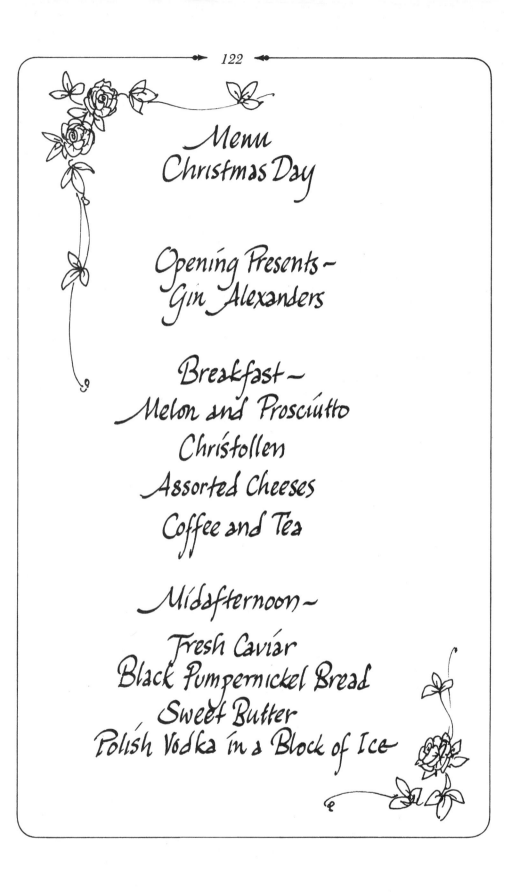

Menu
Christmas Day

Opening Presents —
Gin Alexanders

Breakfast —
Melon and Prosciutto
Christollen
Assorted Cheeses
Coffee and Tea

Midafternoon —
Fresh Caviar
Black Pumpernickel Bread
Sweet Butter
Polish Vodka in a Block of Ice

Dinner~

Crudités

Turkey
Plain and Oyster Stuffing
Mashed Potatoes and Gravy
Creamed Leeks
Cranberry Sauce

Wine

Sherbet

Mincemeat Pie
Coffee
Brandy

Gin Alexanders

To make one cocktail: Combine 1 ounce of crème de cacao, 2 ounces of gin, ½ ounce (1 tablespoon) of heavy cream, and 3 to 4 ice cubes in a mixing glass. Set the shaker on top of the mixing glass and, grasping them firmly together with both hands, shake vigorously 7 or 8 times. Strain and pour into cocktail glasses.

This cocktail is served Christmas morning and Larry uses one-half the amount of gin in the recipe so that we may all keep our bright shining heads.

Christollen

Scald 2 cups of milk and add 1 cup sugar, 2 teaspoons salt and 1⅓ cups butter. Stir until the butter is melted and let cool to lukewarm. Add 2 yeast cakes or 2 envelopes of dry yeast dissolved in a little lukewarm water, and stir in 2 cups of flour. Let the batter rest in a warm place until it is bubbly. Then stir in 4 eggs, beaten, and about 6 cups of flour, or enough to make a light but not sticky dough.

Knead in 1½ cups each of chopped blanched almonds and raisins softened in a little hot water and thoroughly drained; ½ cup each of chopped citron and currants; ¼ cup each of candied cherries and chopped candied pineapple; 1 tablespoon of candied orange peel; the grated rind of 1 lemon and 2 teaspoons of vanilla. Continue to knead the dough until it is smooth and elastic.

Cover the dough lightly and let it rise in a warm place until double in bulk. Punch the dough down, divide it into three parts, and let the parts rest for 10 minutes. Flatten each part into an oval about ¾-inch thick, brush with melted butter and sprinkle lightly with sugar and cinnamon. Fold the ovals not quite in half (like large Parker House rolls), pinch the ends firmly together and place the loaves on oiled baking sheets.

Brush the loaves with melted butter again and let them rise for about 1 hour, or until double in bulk. Bake in hot oven, 425° F., for 10 minutes, reduce the oven temperature to 350° F. and continue to bake for 40 minutes longer. Cool, glaze with confectioners' sugar icing and decorate with large pieces of fruit and nuts.

Vodka Frozen in Ice

We like Polish or Russian vodka. Save a gallon plastic jug: a milk container or the kind apple juice comes in at an orchard. Cut the handle and mouth off the jug, leaving a plastic tub. (You can use a plastic tub, but for some reason I always trim a jug. Maybe a good reason is that it will be destroyed and why waste a plastic tub?) Put the bottle of vodka into the center of the tub, fill the tub with water, and put the whole thing into the freezer and freeze it. When serving, cut away the plastic to leave the block of ice. Be sure that you have left enough of the neck of the bottle exposed to enable you to pour when you cut away the plastic. If the ice block is too high on the bottle there will not be enough neck to grasp.

Turkey with Plain and Oyster Stuffing

Prepare the turkey by rubbing it all over and inside the cavity with salt and pepper and a cut lemon.

Stuffing Plan to use about ¾ cup of stuffing for every pound of bird's dressed weight.

The night before roasting the turkey, cut good quality white bread into cubes: one or two loaves, depending on the size of the turkey (I leave the crust on the bread). Leave to "stale" overnight. We spread the bread cubes out on a cloth on a large table to get as much air as possible and, from time to time, roll them around a bit.

The next day, chop the parsley, celery, and celery leaves (a good bit of this, depending on the amount of stuffing), and melt a lot of butter in a big skillet (you will probably want ¾ to 1 pound of butter for a largish turkey). Add the celery and parsley to the butter and cook gently for a few minutes. Put the bread cubes in a very large bowl and pour the melted butter and celery and parsley over them. Salt and pepper well, and mix it all together with your hands, tossing the butter through the stuffing. Put a little of the bread into the skillet to mop up the remaining butter. You can now stuff the neck cavity with the "plain" stuffing, if you wish—for those who may not care for oysters, or just for variety.

To the rest of the stuffing add the drained raw oysters (a dozen or more, depending upon taste and the size of the bird) and some of the oyster liquor so that the bread becomes moistened with it. The bread should not be soggy, just slightly moistened through and still springy to the touch. Stuff the big cavity with this dressing, packing it in well, but not too tightly, to allow for expansion. Then place a crust of bread over the opening and truss the bird, tying the legs and wings to the body. Put slices of butter on the breast, legs and other parts of the body. With a lid or foil, cover and bake in a 350° F. oven about 18 minutes per pound. One hour before the turkey is done, uncover it, allowing it to brown.

To tell when the turkey is done, I always look at the legs; when they pull away from the body so that it looks as though only skin is stretched across the gap, it is ready.

Gravy While the turkey is cooking, simmer the neck and giblets in water for about 1 hour until tender. Set aside to cool. When the turkey has finished cooking, remove it from the roaster and place it on its serving platter to rest. Put the roaster on the stove over two burners, moderate heat, and add the potato water (saved from the potatoes cooked for mashed potatoes) and the broth from the cooked giblets. Chop the giblets and set them aside. Add more water to the roasting pan if necessary and bring this to a boil. Make a paste of flour and water (perhaps 1 cup of flour, to which you add slowly—stirring —enough water to make a thin sauce. Make sure this is smooth by beating it with a fork or whisk. Then add it, little by little, stirring always, to the juices in the roasting pan. Stir until the gravy is as thick as you want it—I don't like it too thick—then let it simmer over a very low flame a few more minutes to "cook" the flour. Add the chopped giblets to heat through, and salt and pepper, and serve with the turkey.

Mashed Potatoes

Peel the potatoes and boil them until just tender. Drain and put them through a ricer or food mill into a large bowl. Heat enough milk to make the potatoes smooth and creamy. Add a lot of sweet butter to the potatoes, and salt and pepper. Pour

the hot milk—little by little—into the potatoes, whipping all the while. Check for seasoning and serve.

potato ricer

Boil an onion or shallots with the potatoes and rice it into the mixture. Or a few turnips or parsnips.

Chopped chives or dill garnish the potatoes at the end of the whipping.

Creamed Vegetables: Leeks or Small Onions

We couldn't get pearl onions last year—someone had bought them all—so I bought a lot of leeks; we cleaned them carefully and creamed them. I think they were better than onions, certainly as good—a matter of taste.

For 1 cup of white sauce or béchamel sauce, use 2 tablespoons of unsalted butter and 2 tablespoons of unbleached flour. Melt the butter in a saucepan (do not brown it), and stir in the flour to make a roux. Gradually add 1 cup of milk to the roux, stirring as you add it and as it thickens over a very low flame. Less milk

will make a richer sauce, more milk a thinner one. This is a classic sauce and has endless variations. I put in a few dashes of Tabasco and season the sauce further with salt and freshly ground white pepper.

I like the vegetables to stand in the sauce awhile to blend together. The lowest heat must be used with a "flame tamer" to keep it from scorching. If the sauce thickens more than desired, add a small amount of the vegetable water to thin and flavor it.

My mother served cauliflower with cheese sauce at Christmas dinner. The basic béchamel is made, and cheese is grated into it and allowed to melt. Sprinkle some sweet Hungarian paprika over the sauce. Slightly more milk is probably needed to thin the sauce a little to compensate for the cheese.

Cranberry Sauce

This year I had an hilarious time with the cranberry sauce. I dutifully made it Christmas Eve day and put it outside the kitchen door to cool (the ice box was full). There is a post outside the kitchen door which is inaccessible to raccoons and other such imps! I left it for the night. This year it rained on Christmas Day. Just before serving dinner I went to fetch the cranberry sauce—which was now filled with water, the berries afloat. I had placed the bowl just under the rain spout! I drained off the water, and served the sauce to company who commented upon its delightful freshness. I don't know how this could be repeated. Use rain water? rinse the sauce with rain water? stir in some snow? The moral is: just get on with it.

Boil together 1 scant cup of sugar to 1 cup of water for each quart of cranberries. Let the syrup cook a little until it is well blended, and then add 1 quart of cranberries that have been washed and cleaned (stems removed, less than perfect berries discarded). Cook them in the syrup until they just begin to pop, less than 10 minutes. Then add to the sauce 3 or 4 cloves, 3 or 4 sticks of cinnamon one inch long, and some freshly grated nutmeg. Let this cool and then refrigerate.

I like cranberry sauce served in glass or crystal bowls, preferably bowls on a pedestal.

Alex and Nile's Sherbet

We first had this sherbet at Alex's at Thanksgiving to clear the palate and refresh the appetite between the main course and dessert. It worked so well, and was so good and such a nice moment of pause in the meal, that we've adopted it for our Christmas dinner.

Alex says this is a dry sherbet, not a sweet one, unless you sweeten it to have for dessert. In the summer use fresh berries when they're in season. In the winter use your own frozen berries or commercially frozen ones. For Christmas dinner I bring some wild cranberries, frozen or jarred, from the island in Maine.

Put 2 packages or 1 quart of berries through a strainer, making a thick puree. In a saucepan dissolve ½ cup of sugar and 2 teaspoons of gelatin in a cup of boiling water; stir it well. To this add 2 tablespoons of lemon juice (or lime juice) and 1 pint of Cassis (or more). Whisk it all in a bowl or blend it and pour it into a mold or an ice cube tray. Put it in the freezer.

Check the sherbet in about an hour, and when it is slushy, whisk it again. Allow to set for another half hour and serve. To make ahead, remove it from the freezer to the refrigerator an hour before serving.

Pastry Dough for the Mincemeat Pie

Into a big bowl put 1½ cups flour, ¼ pound of butter cut into small pieces, and 3 tablespoons of chilled vegetable shortening. Use a pastry blender or your fingertips to quickly "chop" the flour and fats into the consistency of coarse meal. Dissolve a pinch of salt in ⅓ cup of ice water and pour it into the flour and fat mixture. Blend this into a ball with your fingertips or a rubber spatula. Put the ball onto a table or slab of marble and smoosh bits of it along the board with the heel of your hand to finally blend it. With the spatula scoop it up and gently make it into a ball again. Wrap this in waxed paper and chill it in the refrigerator or freezer before rolling it out.

Christmas Carols

L. R.

Ever since the children were very small, we have always sung carols around the piano at Christmastime. Later on it became a bit more elaborate, with the occasional addition of a flute or guitar obbligato from one of the girls and sometimes, if there are a few more men to help, we may sing in harmony—even in four parts. But most of the time it's just plain old unison with piano accompaniment, nothing fancy, and everyone seems to love it.

There are about two dozen carols which have, over the centuries, become a permanent fixture in the American Christmas scene. They are endlessly heard in all the media from street bands or strolling carolers, and also these days in banks, on ski slopes and in elevators. Still, we sing them all at home—and

with great pleasure—because, however overexposed, they are ever beautiful and evoke unfailingly the special spirit of the holiday in both its sacred and secular aspects.

But, of course, this group of well-known carols is only a narrow segment of the great body of popular Christmas music sung all over the world. So, from various sources and different cultures, many less familiar but equally wonderful songs have gradually joined our holiday repertory. Maria would bring them back from school in England, or I would find them in old collections. One I heard from the bagpiping shepherds who come down every Christmas from the Italian hills to sing and play in the streets of Rome.

The little sampling that follows can hardly, however, be called esoteric. It is simply a group of carols we like a lot, less famous in America than in the countries of their origin. Some readers will recognize a few of them, some perhaps all, others may find them all new. In any case, they are not likely to be heard on the average television Christmas special.

The tunes are a mixed bag. A few go back a century or two, others six or seven. All are timeless and beautiful. The harmonizations are mostly personal, what my fingers happen to find on the keyboard.

Sing we now Noël!

Past Three a Clock

G. R. Woodward

Tune: "London Waits"

Lively

Past three a clock, And a cold-fros-ty morn-ing: Past three a clock; Good mor-row, mas-ters all!

fine

1. Born is a ba — by, Gen-tle as
2. Se-raph quire sing-eth. An-gel bell

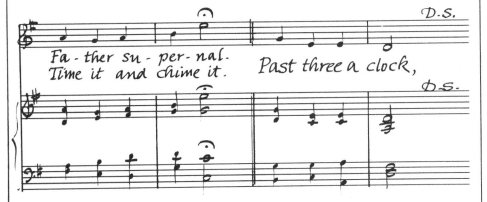

may be, Son — of — th'e — ter — nal
ring-eth: Hark — how — they — rime it,

Fa - ther su - per - nal.
Time it and chime it.

Past three a clock,

D.S.

3. Mid earth rejoices
   Hearing such voices
   Ne'erbefore so well
   Carolling Nowell,
      Past three a clock, etc.

4. Cheese from the dairy
   Bring they for Mary,
   And, not for money,
   Butter and honey.
      Past three a clock, etc.

5. Light out of star-land
   Leadeth from far land.
   Princes to meet him
   Worship and greet him.
      Past three a clock, etc.

6. Thus they: I pray you,
   Up, sirs, nor stay you,
   Till ye confess him
   Likewise, and bless him.
      Past three a clock, etc.

This Endris Night

15th Century English Carol

Tranquil and flowing

1. This en-dris night I saw a sight A
2. This love-ly la-dy sat and sung, And

star as bright as day; And
to her Child did say: "My

e'er a-mong a mai-den sung, "Lul-
son, my bro-ther, fa-ther dear, Why

lay,   bye bye, lul -   lay."_____
liest   thou thus in   hay?"_____

3. The child then spake in His talking
   And to His mother said:
   "Yea, I am known as heaven king,
   In crib though I be laid."

4. "For angels bright down to me light:
   Thou knowest 'tis no nay:
   And for this sight thou may'st delight
   To sing, 'bye bye lullay.'"

Rocking

Czech Carol
("Hajej nynjej")

With gentle movement

mp

1. Lit-tle Je-sus, sweet-ly sleep, do not stir;
2. Ma-ry's lit-tle ba-by, Sleep, sweet-ly sleep,

We will lend a coat of fur, We will rock you
Sleep in com-fort, slum-ber deep; We will rock you

rock you, rock you, We will rock you, rock you, rock you, See the fur to
rock you, rock you, We will rock you, rock you, rock you, We will serve you

Keep you warm, Smug-ly round your ti'-ny form.
all we can, Dar-ling, dar-ling lit-tle man.

'Ding Dong! Merrily On High

G. R. Woodward

16th Century French tune

With spirit

1. Ding dong! mer-ri-ly on high in heav'n the bells are ring-ing:
2. E'en so here be-low be-low Let stee-ple bells be swung-en,
3. Pray you du-ti-ful-ly prime your ma-tin chime ye ring-ers;

Ding dong! ve-ri-ly the sky is riv'n with an-gel sing-ing.
And i - o, i-o, i - o, *) by priest and peo-ple sung-en.
May you beau-ti-ful-ly rime your eve-time Song ye sing-ers.

Glo - - - - - -

*) i-o pronounced ee-o

- - - - - - - ri-a, Ho-san-na in ex - cel - sis!

The Sleep of the Infant Jesus

Traditional French Carol

Quietly sustained

1. Here 'twixt the ass and ox - en mild,
1. En - tre le boeuf et l'â - ne gris,

pp

Sleep, Sleep, sleep, Thou lit-tle child:
Dors, dors, dors le pe-tit fils:

REFRAIN.

An-gels pure and white Guard Thee thro' the night,
Mille an-ges di - vins, Mil-le se-ra-phins,

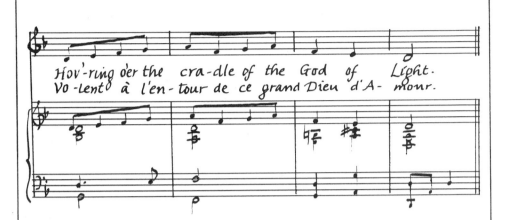

Hov'-ring o'er the cra-dle of the God of Light.
Vo-lent à l'en-tour de ce grand Dieu d'A-mour.

2. Here, with the rose
   and lily bright,
   Sleep, sleep, sleep
   Thou little Child:

   REFRAIN

2. Entre les roses
   et les lys,
   Dors, dors, dors
   le petit fils :

   REFRAIN

3. Here, 'mid the shepherd's
   great delight
   Sleep, sleep, sleep
   Thou little Child

   REFRAIN

3. Entre les pastoureaux
   jolis,
   Dors, dors, dors
   le petit fils :

   REFRAIN

The Eve of Christmas

English Carol

Moderately fast.

1. In the sky the stars are shim-mer-ing;
2. On the tree the can-dles glis-ten-ing;

This is the Eve of Christ - mas.
This is the Eve of Christ - mas.

Fields of snow in moon-light glim-mer-ing;
Chil-dren to the Sto - ry lis-ten-ing;

This is the Eve of Christ - mas. The
This is the Eve of Christ - mas. The

i - ci - cles hang from roof and wall, and
Hea-ven-ly birth brings joy to all, and

this is the Eve of Christ - mas.
this is the Eve of Christ - mas.

Dormi, dormi, O bel bambin

Traditional Italian

Tenderly

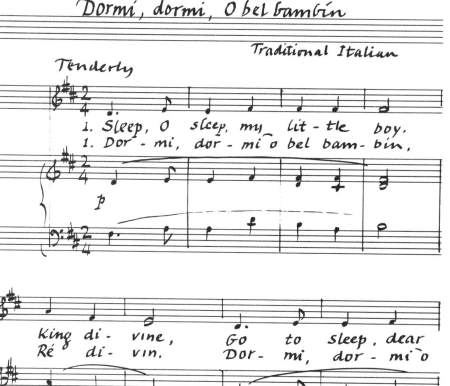

1. Sleep, O sleep, my lit - tle boy.
1. Dor - mi, dor - mi o bel bam - bin,

King di - vine,   Go   to   sleep , dear
Ré di - vin.   Dor- mi,   dor - mi o

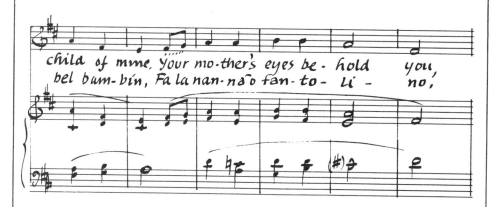

child of mine, your mo-ther's eyes be- hold   you,
bel bum-bin, Fa la nan-na o fan-to- li -   no,

fair-est child, ho-ly child, your-
Ré di - vin, Ré di - vin, Fa la

rit.

mo-ther's arms en-fold you
nan-na o fan-to-li - no.

rit.

2. Dearest love, why do you weep?
   Go to sleep
   Close your eyes in slumber deep,
   O Prince of joy and sorrow.
   Fairest child, holy child
   Sleep softly till the morrow.

2. Perché piangi, o mio tresor?
   Dolce amor,
   Perché piangi, o mio tresor?
   Fa la nanna, o caro figlio,
   Tanto bel, tanto bel,
   Fa la nanna, o caro figlio.

Once in Royal David's City

Cecil F. Alexander, 1848 Henry J. Gauntlett, 1858

Moving moderately

1. Once in roy - al Da - vid's ci - ty Stood a low - ly cat - tle shed, where a mo - ther laid her ba - by, In a man - ger for his
2. He came down to earth - from hea - ven, Who is God and Lord - of - all, And his shel - ter was a sta - ble, And his cra - dle was a

bed :   Ma—ry   was   that mo—ther
stall :   With the   poor   and mean and

mild, — Je-sus Christ her lit-tle   child .
low-ly , Lived on earth our Sa-viour ho-ly.

3. And our eyes at last shall
    see him
Through his own redeeming
    love,
For that child so dear and
    gentle
Is our Lord in heaven
    above;
And he leads his children
    on
To the place where he is
    gone .

4. Not in that poor lowly
    stable ,
With the oxen standing
    by .
We shall see him : but
    in heaven
Set at God's right hand
    on high.
Where like stars his
    children crowned
All in white shall
    wait around .

Joseph Dearest

14th Century German Folksong

Swaying gently

1. Jo-seph dear-est, Jo-seph mild,
1. Jo-seph, lie-ber, Jo-seph mein,

p

Help me rock my lit - tle child.
Hilf mir wie-gen mein Kin - de - lein,

God will give you your re-ward in
Gott, der wird dein Loh - ner sein im

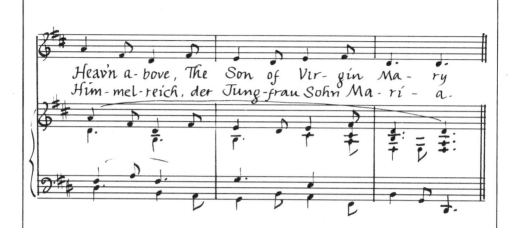

Heav'n a-bove, The Son of Vir-gin Ma-ry
Him-mel-reich, der Jung-frau Sohn Ma-ri-a.

2. Gladly, dearest
    Mary mine,
    I will rock your
    "Kindelein,"
    God will give me
    my reward
    In Heav'n above,
    The Child of Virgin
    Mary.

2. Gerne, liebe Muhme
    mein,
    helf ich Dir wiegen
    Dein Kindelein,
    dass Gott müsse
    mein Lohner sein
    im Himmelreich,
    der Jungfrau Sohn
    Maria.

Noël Nouvelet

With a moderate swing

Tune: Old Provençale
("Ave Maris Stella")

1. No-ël nou-ve-let, O let us sing No-el!
1. No-ël nou-ve-let, No-ël chan-tons i-ci,

Glo — ry to God! Now let your prai-ses swell!
De — vo-tés gens, cri — ons à-Dieu mer-ci!

REFRAIN.

Sing we NO-el for Christ the new-born King, No-el!
Chan-tons NO-ël pour le roi nou-ve-let, No-ël!

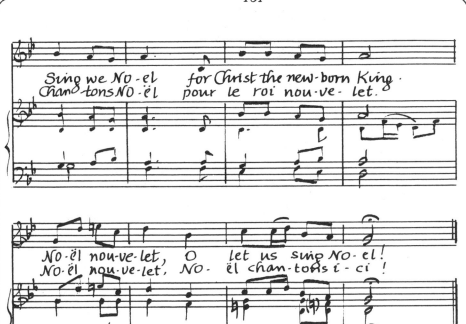

Sing we No-el for Christ the new-born King.
Chan-tons No-ël pour le roi nou-ve-let.

No-ël nou-ve-let, O let us sing No-el!
No-ël nou-ve-let, No-ël chan-tons i-ci!

2. Angels did say, "O shepherds,
   come and see,
   Born in Bethlehem, a blessed
   Lamb for thee.
   REFRAIN

3. In the manger bed, the
   shepherds found the Child;
   Joseph was there, and
   Mother Mary mild.
   REFRAIN

4. Soon came the kings from
   following the star,
   Bearing costly gifts from
   Eastern lands afar.
   REFRAIN

5. Brought to Him gold and
   incense of great price;
   Then the stable bare
   resembled Paradise.
   REFRAIN

2. L'Ange disait, "pasteurs,
   partez d'ici!
   En Bethléem trouverez
   l'agnelet.
   REFRAIN

3. En Bethléem, étant
   tous réunis,
   Trouverent l'enfant,
   Joseph, Marie aussi.
   REFRAIN

4. Bientôt, les Rois, par
   l'étoile éclaircis,
   A Bethléem vinrent
   une matinée.
   REFRAIN

5. L'un portait l'or,
   l'autre l'encens bém;
   L'étable alors au
   Paradis semblait.
   REFRAIN

The Friendly Beasts

Robert Davis

12th Century French Carol

Quietly moving

1. Je-sus our bro-ther, kind and good, Was
2. "I", said the cow, all white and red, "I
3. "I", said the dove from the raf-ters high, "I

hum-bly born in a sta-ble rude, And the friend-ly beasts a-
gave him my man-ger for his bed, I gave him my hay to
cooed him to sleep so he would not cry, We cooed him to sleep, my

round him stood. Je-sus our bro-ther, kind and good.
pil-low his head." "I," said the cow, all white and red.
mate and I." "I," said the dove from the raf-ters high.

My Dancing Day

Traditional English Carol

With a lilt, brightly

1. To-mor-row shall be - my danc-ing day: I
2. Then was - I born of a vir - gin pure, Of

would - my true - love so - did chance to see the le - gend
her - I took - flesh-ly sub-stance; Thus was I knit to

Of my play, To call my true-love to — my dance:
man's - na-ture, To call my true-love to — my dance:

REFRAIN.

Sing O my love, O - my love, my love, my love; This have I done - for my - true love.

3. In a manger laid and
    wrapped I was,
   So very poor, this
    was my chance.
   Betwixt an ox and a
    silly poor ass,
   To call my true love
    to my dance:

      Sing O my love, etc.

4. Then afterwards baptized
    I was:
   The Holy Ghost on me
    did glance,
   My Father's voice
    heard from above
   To call my true love
    to my dance:

      Sing O my love, etc.

Conversation About Christmas
by Dylan Thomas

SMALL BOY: Years and years ago, when you were a boy . . .

SELF: When there were wolves in Wales, and birds the colour of red-flannel petticoats whisked past the harp-shaped hills, when we sang and wallowed all night and day in caves that smelt like Sunday afternoons in damp front farmhouse parlours, and chased, with the jawbones of deacons, the English and the bears . . .

SMALL BOY: You are not so old as Mr. Beynon Number Twenty-Two who can remember when there were no motors. Years and years ago, when you were a boy . . .

SELF: Oh, before the motor even, before the wheel, before the duchess-faced horse, when we rode the daft and happy hills bareback . . .

SMALL BOY: You're not so daft as Mrs. Griffiths up the street, who says she puts her ear under the water in the reservoir and listens to the fish talk Welsh. When you were a boy, what was Christmas like?

SELF: It snowed.

SMALL BOY: It snowed last year, too. I made a snowman and my brother knocked it down and I knocked my brother down and then we had tea.

SELF: But that was not the same snow. Our snow was not only shaken in whitewash buckets down the sky, I think it came shawling out of the ground and swam and drifted out of the arms and hands and bodies of the trees; snow grew overnight on the roofs of the houses like a pure and grandfather moss, minutely ivied the walls, and settled on the postman, opening the gate, like a dumb, numb thunderstorm of white, torn Christmas cards.

SMALL BOY: Were there postmen, then, too?

SELF: With sprinkling eyes and wind-cherried noses, on spread, frozen feet they crunched up to the doors and mittened on them manfully. But all that the children could hear was a ringing of bells.

SMALL BOY: You mean that the postman went rat-a-tat-tat and the doors rang?

SELF: The bells that the children could hear were inside them.

SMALL BOY: I only hear thunder sometimes, never bells.

SELF: There were church bells, too.

SMALL BOY: Inside them?

SELF: No, no, no, in the bat-black, snow-white belfries, tugged by bishops and storks. And they rang their tidings over the bandaged town, over the frozen foam of the powder and ice-cream hills, over the crackling sea. It seemed that all the churches boomed, for joy, under my window; and the weather-cocks crew for Christmas, on our fence.

SMALL BOY: Get back to the postmen.

SELF: They were just ordinary postmen, fond of walking, and dogs, and Christmas, and the snow. They knocked on the doors with blue knuckles ...

SMALL BOY: Ours has got a black knocker ...

SELF: And then they stood on the white welcome mat in the little, drifted porches, and clapped their hands together, and huffed and puffed, making ghosts with their breath, and jogged from foot to foot like small boys wanting to go out.

SMALL BOY: And then the Presents?

SELF: And then the Presents, after the Christmas box. And the cold postman, with a rose on his button-nose, tingled down the teatray-slithered run of the chilly glinting hill. He went in his ice-bound boots like a man on fishmonger's slabs. He wagged

his bag like a frozen camel's hump, dizzily turned the corner on one foot, and, by God, he was gone.

SMALL BOY: Get back to the Presents.

SELF: There were the Useful Presents: engulfing mufflers of the old coach days, and mittens made for giant sloths; zebra scarves of a substance like silky gum that could be tug-o'-warred down to the goloshes; blinding tam-o'-shanters like patchwork tea-cosies, and bunny-scutted busbies and balaclavas for victims of head-shrinking tribes; from aunts who always wore wool next to the skin, there were moustached and rasping vests that made you wonder why the aunties had any skin left at all; and once I had a little crocheted nose-bag from an aunt now, alas, no longer whinnying with us. And pictureless books in which small boys, though warned, with quotations, not to, *would* skate on Farmer Garge's pond, and did, and drowned; and books that told me everything about the wasp, except why.

SMALL BOY: Get on to the Useless Presents.

SELF: On Christmas Eve I hung at the foot of my bed Bessie Bunter's black stocking, and always, I said, I would stay awake all the moonlit, snowlit night to hear the roof-alighting reindeer and see the hollied boot descend through soot. But soon the sand of the snow drifted into my eyes, and, though I stared towards the fireplace and around the flickering room where the black sack-like stocking hung, I was asleep before the chimney trembled and the room was red and white with Christmas. But in the morning, though no snow melted on the bedroom floor, the stocking bulged and brimmed: press it, it squeaked like a mouse-in-a-box; it smelt of tangerine; a furry arm lolled over, like the arm of a kangaroo out of its mother's belly; squeeze it hard in the middle, and something squelched; squeeze it again —squelch again. Look out of the frost-scribbled window: on the great loneliness of the small hill, a blackbird was silent in the snow.

SMALL BOY: Were there any sweets?

SELF: Of course there were sweets. It was the marshmallows that squelched. Hardboileds, toffee, fudge and allsorts, crunches, cracknels, humbugs, glaciers, and marzipan and butterwelsh for the Welsh. And troops of bright tin soldiers who, if they would not fight, could always run. And Snakes-and-Fami-

lies and Happy Ladders. And Easy Hobbi-Games for Little Engineers, complete with Instructions. Oh, easy for Leonardo! And a whistle to make the dogs bark to wake up the old man next door to make him beat on the wall with his stick to shake our picture off the wall. And a packet of cigarettes: you put one in your mouth and you stood at the corner of the street and you waited for hours, in vain, for an old lady to scold you for smoking a cigarette and then, with a smirk, you ate it. And, last of all, in the toe of the stocking, sixpence like a silver corn. And then downstairs for breakfast under the balloons!

SMALL BOY: Were there Uncles, like in our house?

SELF: There are always Uncles at Christmas. The same Uncles. And on Christmas mornings, with dog-disturbing whistle and sugar fags, I would scour the swathed town for the news of the little world, and find always a dead bird by the white Bank or by the deserted swings: perhaps a robin, all but one of his fires out, and that fire still burning on his breast. Men and women wading and scooping back from church or chapel, with taproom noses and wind-smacked cheeks, all albinos, huddled their stiff black jarring feathers against the irreligious snow. Mistletoe hung from the gas in all the front parlours; there was sherry and walnuts and bottled beer and crackers by the dessertspoons; and cats in their fur-abouts watched the fires; and the high-heaped fires crackled and spat, all ready for the chestnuts and the mulling pokers. Some few large men sat in the front parlours, without their collars, Uncles almost certainly, trying their new cigars, holding them out judiciously at arm's-length, returning them to their mouths, coughing, then holding them out again as though waiting for the explosion; and some few small aunts, not wanted in the kitchen, nor anywhere else for that matter, sat on the very edges of their chairs, poised and brittle, afraid to break, like faded cups and saucers. Not many those mornings trod the piling streets: an old man always, fawn-bowlered, yellow-gloved, and, at this time of year, with spats of snow, would take his constitutional to the white bowling-green, and back, as he would take it wet or fine on Christmas Day or Doomsday; sometimes two hale young men, with big pipes blazing, no overcoats, and windblown scarves, would trudge, unspeaking, down to the forlorn sea, to work up an appetite, to

blow away the fumes, who knows, to walk into the waves until nothing of them was left but the two curling smoke clouds of their inextinguishable briars.

SMALL BOY: Why didn't you go home for Christmas dinner?

SELF: Oh, but I did, I always did. I would be slapdashing home, the gravy smell of the dinners of others, the bird smell, the brandy, the pudding and mince, weaving up my nostrils, when out of a snow-clogged side-lane would come a boy the spit of myself, with a pink-tipped cigarette and the violet past of a black eye, cocky as a bullfinch, leering all to himself. I hated him on sight and sound, and would be about to put my dog-whistle to my lips and blow him off the face of Christmas when suddenly he, with a violet wink, put *his* whistle to *his* lips and blew so stridently, so high, so exquisitely loud, that gobbling faces, their cheeks bulged with goose, would press against their tinselled windows, the whole length of the white echoing street.

SMALL BOY: What did you have for Dinner?

SELF: Turkey, and blazing pudding.

SMALL BOY: Was it nice?

SELF: It was not made on earth.

SMALL BOY: What did you do after dinner?

SELF: The Uncles sat in front of the fire, took off their collars, loosened all buttons, put their large moist hands over their watch-chains, groaned a little, and slept. Mothers, aunts, and sisters scuttled to and fro, bearing tureens. The dog was sick. Auntie Beattie had to have three aspirins, but Auntie Hannah, who liked port, stood in the middle of the snowbound backyard, singing like a big-bosomed thrush. I would blow up balloons to see how big they would blow up to; and, when they burst, which they all did, the Uncles jumped and rumbled. In the rich and heavy afternoon, the Uncles breathing like dolphins and the snow descending, I would sit in the front room, among festoons and Chinese lanterns, and nibble at dates, and try to make a model man-o'-war, following the Instructions for Little Engineers, and produce what might be mistaken for a sea-going tram. And then, at Christmas tea, the recovered Uncles would be jolly over their mince-pies; and the great iced cake loomed in the centre of the table like a marble grave. Auntie Hannah laced her tea with rum, because it was only once a year. And in the evening, there was Music. An uncle played the fiddle, a

cousin sang Cherry Ripe, and another uncle sang Drake's Drum. It was very warm in the little house. Auntie Hannah, who had got on to the parsnip wine, sang a song about Rejected Love, and Bleeding Hearts, and Death, and then another in which she said that her Heart was like a Bird's Nest; and then everybody laughed again, and then I went to bed. Looking through my bedroom window, out into the moonlight and the flying, unending, smoke-coloured snow, I could see the lights in the windows of all the other houses on our hill, and hear the music rising from them up the long, steadily falling night. I turned the gas down, I got into bed, I said some words to the close and holy darkness, and then I slept.

SMALL BOY: But it all sounds like an ordinary Christmas.

SELF: It was.

SMALL BOY: But Christmas when you were a boy wasn't any different to Christmas now.

SELF: It was, it was.

SMALL BOY: Why was Christmas different then?

SELF: I mustn't tell you.

SMALL BOY: Why mustn't you tell me? Why is Christmas different for me?

SELF: I mustn't tell you.

SMALL BOY: Why can't Christmas be the same for me as it was for you when you were a boy?

SELF: I mustn't tell you. I mustn't tell you because it is Christmas now.

6

Christmas Week

Boxing Day

I've always been curious about the origin of the name Boxing Day, with dim visions of prizefighters, and what in the world does that have to do with the winter solstice or the birthday of Jesus? Nothing. Boxing Day comes from England, when the alms boxes in churches were opened the day after Christmas, or from pottery boxes that were carried round the countryside by apprentices and filled by householders, and the collected money used for a feast.

Boxing Day belongs to our friend Arnold. I have a vivid picture of him, fairly early in the morning of the day after Christmas, standing in the kitchen with a turkey drumstick in one hand and a glass of wine in the other, all gathered from the Christmas dinner table; "old food" or "used food," he calls it. He greets all with a cheerful "good morning." Our tradition for Boxing Day is an early walk with Arnold in the morning for those who are up, and up to it. Some guests stay on and some leave and the day trails its way. Our dinner menu is usually a pasta marinara and salad and whatever else anyone wants from all the food that is about.

We have a party during Christmas week to which we invite the friends who cannot come on Christmas Day because of their own traditional events. In planning the menu for this party, I try to find things that will not be too much work because it is such a busy week anyway. I order for the party at the same time that I place the whole Christmas order, so that all is done well ahead. The house is already festive, the plans are all made and so the execution is relatively easy.

Menu
Boxing Day Dinner

Pasta all'Arrabbiata
Salad

Red Wine

Fresh Pears and Gorgonzola

Fruitcake
Coffee

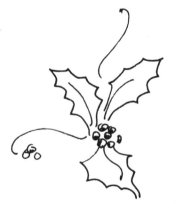

Pasta all'Arrabbiata

In a large stainless-steel or enameled skillet, brown 3 or 4 finely chopped cloves of garlic in olive oil (about ⅓ cup, or to taste). Add a liberal pinch of Italian hot peppers or 2 pods of hot red peppers, chopped. Simmer a minute or two, stirring, before adding a large can of Italian tomatoes (or 1 quart of your own home-canned pear tomatoes). Use a wooden spoon and chop or break up the tomatoes while they are cooking. Season this with a generous pinch of basil and oregano and some chopped parsley. Mix together well and continue cooking gently for a few more minutes.

Now add a medium-size can of tuna fish, which you have drained. Use a fork to chop the tuna into small pieces after it has been added to the sauce.

Cook the sauce for about 1 hour, simmering gently. Check the seasoning and serve with pasta.

Salads

Wash and dry the lettuce. The new salad dryers that spin the lettuce are great. This can be done in advance. Wrap the greens in a linen towel and put them into the refrigerator until the last minute before serving. Sometimes I like to use just one kind of greenery and sometimes a mixture: I am especially fond of arugola and watercress. The elements of a salad are numerous. There was a birthday salad with violets, raw mushrooms and walnuts. With duck I like Boston lettuce, grapefruit wedges and red onion slices. At the Christmas Party a dark green lettuce with pomegranate seeds scattered through it ornaments the season.

Dressing: Mash a clove of garlic (or part of a clove—a question of taste) with salt in the bottom of the salad bowl. Add one tablespoon of wine vinegar and freshly ground black pepper. At this point a good mustard (either dry or prepared) may be added. Also lemon juice can substitute for the vinegar, depending on the menu. Then add three tablespoons of good oil. Olive oil, or a mixture of oils: olive oil, safflower oil or sunflower oil.

The Christmas Week Party

This year we had Cherry-glazed Ham, Cheese Charlotte, Escalloped Tomatoes (made from my freshly canned ones), and Corn Bread, exactly as the Los Angeles Museum's cookbook suggests. Their cookbook is called *Entertaining Is an Art* and it is one of my favorites. Dessert is never a problem. There are the Black and White Fruitcakes, all the Christmas cookies, lots of fresh fruit and, this year, Nadia's cake, Dobos Torte, made from a recipe in *The Cuisine of Hungary* that she gave me for Christmas. It's a beautiful six-layered cake and very, very good.

Last year the menu was Little Meatballs with freshly made noodles, and a big green salad with some pomegranate seeds scattered into it to go with Christmas.

Punches and Christmas Drinks

Sir Edward Kennel, who was the Commander-in-Chief of the English navy, made a huge punch for his ships' crews. The date was 25 October 1599. It was made in a great marble bowl. The recipe: 80 casks of brandy, 9 casks of water, 25,000 limes, 80 pints of lemon juice, 1,300 pounds of sugar, 5 pounds of nutmeg and 300 biscuits and a large cask of Malaga. Six thousand guests were served by the ships' boys, but the fumes were so powerful that the boys had to be replaced every fifteen minutes!

This makes me think of England's Richard II, for whose table 28 oxen, 300 sheep and countless fowls were killed every morning. Or of Mrs. Beeton's recipe which begins "Take the breasts of fifty turkeys . . ."

Maria's Eggnog

Separate 6 eggs and beat the yolks until they are thick and pale and frothy. Add a very scant cup of sugar and beat until the sugar is dissolved. Now add 1½ cups of cognac and blend the mixture together well. Beat the egg whites until they are stiff; then add ½ cup of sugar. Pour the egg yolk mixture into the punch bowl and add to it 1½ cups each of milk and cream,

whisking these before adding them to the bowl. Gently fold in the stiffly beaten egg whites, and sprinkle freshly grated nutmeg over all; then pour in an additional 1½ cups of cognac.

In Pennsylvania we used bourbon instead of cognac and I like it equally well.

Mimosas or Buckshots

Please use freshly squeezed orange juice and a good champagne. The proportions are an individual matter. I like half champagne and half orange juice. Serve them in large crystal goblets if you have them.

Brandy Barnold

Arnold and I concocted these years ago, hence the "Barnold," a contraction of our two first names. For each goblet use 1 cup of milk, ¼ cup of powdered milk, 1 jigger of brandy and honey to taste. Whip these ingredients in a blender, adding crushed ice, and sprinkle some freshly grated nutmeg over the top.

Nutmeg grater

Recipes for Christmas Week

Thelma's Sweet Potato and Marshmallow Casserole

Plan to use approximately 1 sweet potato per person. Scrub and boil the sweet potatoes in salted water until tender. Then peel and mash them, adding sugar and cinnamon to taste, and sweet butter. Cover the bottom of a casserole with a layer of mashed sweet potatoes, and fill the casserole in alternating layers of potatoes and marshmallows, ending with marshmallows.

Bake in a 350° F. oven for 20 to 30 minutes, or just enough to brown the top.

Turkey Soup

At some point remove from the turkey the meat that you want to keep for salad, creamed turkey, or sandwiches, but save the bones and skin. Smash the turkey carcass and put it, with all the bones and skin and the leftover gravy, into a soup pot.

Add water, onion, garlic, salt, peppercorns and simmer for some hours until well cooked. Then cool the broth; pick all remaining meat off the bones and discard them, setting aside the meat.

Heat the broth and add celery, carrots, onions, parsnips, cooked rice (and/or uncooked barley—but not too much as it swells), and simmer all these ingredients in the broth. Then add the turkey meat you have put aside, simmer a few more minutes and taste for seasoning. You can use herbs and other vegetables, whatever you like. I like the taste of several parsnips, chopped, in soups containing barley.

Turkey and Oyster Pie

Drain the liquor from one quart of hand-shucked oysters; bring it to a boil and skim. Line the sides of a baking dish (earthen pottery is good for this) with a rich piecrust dough. Now put in layers of leftover turkey (about 2 to 3 cupfuls) cut in bite-size pieces, and raw oysters. Fill the dish with the turkey and oysters, seasoning each layer with salt, pepper (quite a bit) and bits of butter.

Add the oyster liquor and enough turkey gravy thinned with hot water to bring the liquid even with the top layer. If you

have used all the turkey gravy you can substitute a canned chicken broth.

Cover loosely with enough dough for a thick crust, leaving an opening in the center for the steam to escape. Bake the pie in a moderate oven (preheated to 350° F.) for 40 minutes. Should the liquid evaporate during the baking, add some more of the chicken broth or gravy mixture through the opening.

Cranberry Salad

Dissolve one 3-ounce package of lemon gelatin, one 3-ounce package of cherry gelatin, and ½ cup of sugar in 3 cups of boiling water. Chill until partially set.

While the gelatin is setting, chop up or grind in a blender 2 cups of fresh cranberries and 1 small peeled orange. Dice 1 cup of celery and chop ½ cup of walnuts. Add the fruit and nuts, along with 1 tablespoon of lemon juice and 1 can (8¾ ounces) of crushed pineapple with its juice, to the gelatin mixture when it is partially set. Chill in the refrigerator and cut into squares to serve on a bed of lettuce.

Dish of Snow

This "conceit" is the fantasy of an Elizabethan with the initials A. W. and appears in *A Book of Cookrye* published in England in 1591. It lends itself to a free interpretation, suggests what to do when stuck without a whisk and provides a wonderful image of an apple with a rosemary bush springing from it surrounded all about by billowing fluffy snow and flying cookies! It belongs on the menu of the Mad Hatter's tea party.

Take a pottle [2 quarts] of sweet thick Cream, and the white of eight Eggs, and beate them altogether with a spoone, then put them into your Creme with a dish full of Rosewater, and a dish full of Sugar withall. Then take a stick and make it clean, and then cut it in the end four square, and therwith beat all the aforesaid things together, and ever as it ariseth, take it off, and put it into a Cullender, this doon, take a platter and set an Apple in the midst of it, and stick a thick bush of Rosemary in the Apple. Then cast your Snow upon the Rosemary & fill your platter therwith, and if you have wafers, cast some withall, and so serve them forth.

The New Year

To him that overcometh . . .
I will give him the morning star.

REVELATIONS

Our traditions for the celebration of the old year passing and
the new arriving include watching the old year out with friends
on New Year's Eve, an open house on New Year's Day, and a
family dinner. I read the last book of the Bible, the Revelation
of Saint John the Divine. It's an incredible book, full of imagery
and poetry, and my mother loved it.

We play poker on New Year's Eve to try our luck for the New
Year, a Greek custom. North American Indian tribes on New
Year's light their bonfires, scatter the dead ashes and relight
their fires with great ceremony. The English felt it important
to begin the New Year as you would like it to go on: "To have
plenty of money in your pocket, dine well, rise early, pay your
debts and lend nothing." In my childhood home sausages were
served for New Year's Eve supper because my parents were
going partying and the sausages "coated the stomach." Bell-
ringing, parties, sirens, whistles, all preserve the Saturnalian
wish for an alteration in the accepted patterns of life, for blessed
change. In the morning all the hats and whistles and confetti
from the parties were left on the kitchen table for my pleasure.

My friend Frederick Franck has embraced a Tibetan custom.
Near Warwick, New York, Franck converted an old mill house
over a rushing stream into a chapel. It is a wild and beautiful
place named "Pacem in Terris" (Peace on Earth) and was built
in memory of Pope John XXIII whom Franck knew, loved and
honored. Every New Year's Eve friends gather, bringing the
debris of their year with them; books, food, clothes, records,
anything that for each person denotes attachment. These at-
tachments, debris, are loaded onto a raft which at midnight, is
cut loose from its mooring, symbolizing a letting go of things.
All of last year goes white-water-rafting into the darkness!

New Year's is a movable feast. In ancient Babylon it was
celebrated in what is our March and April; in Egypt it was

linked with the flooding of the Nile; in Europe the New Year was celebrated at different times varying from Christmas to March. January first is a relatively modern innovation connected to the introduction of the Gregorian Calendar in 1582.

It is a turning point, a death and a birth. The old man with the scythe, the infant. It is said that the rites of the New Year correspond to the rites of passage of an individual life. Janus is the Greek god of gates and doors, of beginnings and endings. The month of January, the gateway of the year, is named for him. Janus has two faces, one looking behind and the other looking forward. One looking inward and the other looking outward. The tradition of the New Year resolution (re-solution) is a look at life, a personal hide-and-go-seek. Charles Lamb wrote, "Every first of January that we arrive at, is an imaginary milestone in the turnpike track of human life: at once a resting place for thought and meditation, and a starting place for fresh exertion in the performance of our journey. The man who does not at least *propose to himself* to be better *this* year than he was last, must be either very good or very bad indeed!"

At open house on New Year's Day we serve eggnog and white fruitcake, nuts and a big bowl of mixed fruits. But the culinary event of the day and almost, for me, of the year, is New Year's dinner: roast pork and sauerkraut and mashed potatoes and crudités. The crudités might include gherkins and tiny pickled onions, celery, raw cauliflower, fennel, raw zucchini—it's an improvisation. Buried in the mashed potatoes is a dime to bring good luck for the year to the finder. I adore this meal; the juice from the sauerkraut mingles with the potatoes, the crudités are crisp and refreshing. We drink icy champagne, and for dessert there is a divine Persimmon Pudding.

Janus

Menu
New Year's Day Dinner

Crudités

Roast Pork
Sauerkraut
Mashed Potatoes

Champagne

Jeannie's Persimmon Pudding
Coffee

Roast Pork with Sauerkraut

This is eaten on New Year's Day to bring good luck the whole year through.

Use a rib or loin roast of pork. Bake in a roasting pan that has a cover. Sprinkle the roast with rosemary (fresh if you grow it as a house plant) and bake uncovered at 325° F. according to its size (25–28 minutes per pound at that temperature). An hour before it is done, cover the pork with sauerkraut and its juice. Scatter some juniper berries through the sauerkraut and cover the pan to continue cooking another hour until done. Serve with mashed potatoes and the juices from the roast and sauerkraut.

Note: Do not salt the pork, as the salt from the sauerkraut and its juice will mingle with the juices of the pork to season it.

Jeannie's Persimmon Pudding

Sift together 1 cup of sugar, 1 cup of flour, 2 teaspoons of baking soda and 1 teaspoon of salt.

Add to this dry mixture ⅓ cup of melted butter; 1 egg, 1 cup of ripe persimmon (usually 2 persimmons pureed in the blender), ½ teaspoon of vanilla, and ½ cup of milk. Stir well and place the batter in a greased steamer or form (giving it one sharp rap on the counter top to "settle" the contents) and steam for 1½ hours. Serve hot with sauce.

Note: I generally set the pudding steamer in a tall soup pot, on 3 Mason-jar lids to keep it steady while the water boils. The water should come up halfway on the steamer and should be replaced as it evaporates. The pot should be covered. This pudding can be frozen, thawed out and reheated for about an hour in the steamer.

Sauce Mix together 2 beaten egg yolks and 1 cup of sugar. To this add ½ cup of dry sherry. Just before serving blend in ½ pint of heavy cream, whipped. This is a delicious sauce and may be used with other puddings. Some people eat more sauce than pudding!

This recipe and a steamer were given to Jeannie for an engagement present.

The Lord of Misrule

7

Twelfth Night

Not I, but Christ in me.

SAINT PAUL

As in the progression of nature's seasons, the Christmas Festival needs its own time and tempo to take place. Within the festival, Epiphany is the time for the absorption of all the events. The outer spectacle, including the reunion of family and friends, and all the sparkle and fun and going the whole hog including the postage, contains the question "Why? Why do I do it at all?" And it contains the reply; there is a thread winding through all the events of Christmas, the winter solstice, and the return of the light, that returns us to the awe of the child, the reverence and joy that is part of our nature.

The crescendo of the whole season beginning with Advent, continuing through the Season of the Holy Nights, culminates in Twelfth Night. Twelfth Night, the last of the twelve nights of Christmas, is also called the Feast of Epiphany and Three Kings' Day.

As late as 386 in Antioch the spiritual birth of Christ was celebrated, but the physical birth was not yet established and feasted. The exact date of the birth of Christ has never been determined. In 440, when the church fathers decided upon a date, they chose a day during the time of year that was already celebrated: the winter solstice, the return of the light, the most important festival of the year.

The Greek fathers in the fourteenth century called it the "Day of Lights," referring to the illumination of Jesus at the baptism and also to the light (the Christmas star) that shone in Jordan on Epiphany.

Epiphany is from a Greek word that means "manifestation" or "appearance," signifying the apparition of a divine being, the manifestation of Jesus as Christ the Savior, the light of the world. There were three separate events that were said to have happened on the same day of the year. The first event was the

visit of the three kings with their gifts of gold, frankincense and myrrh. The second was the baptism of Christ by John in the River Jordan, and the third event was the marriage feast at Cana when Christ turned water into wine, proclaiming the miraculous. These events have provided the ingredients for the various celebrations of Twelfth Night as they have evolved through the centuries.

The three kings, named in legend Melchior, Balthazar and Caspar, came from the East bearing precious gifts. They were scholarly priests and are traditionally called Wise Men or Magi. The *magi* were priests of the Zoroastrian sect found among the ancient Medes and Persians. To the ancient Greeks and Hebrews they were astrologers, interpreters of dreams and givers of omens. Melchior, king of Arabia, was the eldest and brought gold to the Christ Child, a king's gift. Balthazar, king of Ethiopia, brought frankincense, symbolizing Christ as high priest. Caspar, king of Tarsus, brought myrrh which was used medicinally and proclaimed Christ as healer-physician. Their way from the East to Bethlehem was lighted by a star. Advent has been likened to the rainbow, Christmas to the sun and Epiphany to the star.

The Christmas star is a powerful image. It has intrigued the world for two thousand years. Was it a heavenly miracle with

its miraculous origins in an astrological event? The Magi were accomplished astrologers and would have recognized an extraordinary grouping of planets. The star shone from the East and guided the Magi to the crib of the Prince of Peace where, in one interpretation, worldly power was surrendered to the divine spiritual authority that was embodied in Christ. Star lore is a strong element in the Nativity event. In Saint Matthew the narrative says, "We have seen His star and we are come to worship Him." The star needed the three kings for its recognition, and the three kings needed the star and its light for guidance.

In Rome, Epiphany was the *Caput festorum* (Chief of Feast). The dictionary says that a feast is a religious festival; a festival is a day of religious feasting! The Roman Twelfth Night was called by a writer of the last century "a perfect witches' sabbath." The Romans crowded the streets with one objective: to make as much noise as possible. They used whistles, horns, drums, tambourines and their lungs to yell and scream! In many lands noisemaking is used to ward off evil spirits and devils.

Magic and the miraculous are tricky things. They can serve the forces of both good and evil, each having its place in life and needing the reconciliatory aspect of real truth. I love the Greek *kallikantzaroi,* goblins much like the Swedish trolls. They have squinty red eyes and little hairy bodies like animals, and they emerge from the earth between Advent and Epiphany with the sole purpose of being pests. But they can be cajoled into being good with sweets and honey cakes because, like the Greeks, they have a sweet tooth!

In Roman Catholic countries now, the Magi are honored on Epiphany. Long ago, children set out to meet the Magi, taking them cakes and figs and hay for their camels. Now the three kings bring gifts to the children as they did to the Infant Jesus. In Mexico the children put their shoes on the window sill so that the kings can fill them with gifts as they pass by. In Spain it is Balthazar, the blackamoor king who fills the children's shoes that they place by the chimney. The Italians have a fairy witch called Befana (a corruption of the word Epiphany). In the legend of the Befana, the three kings passed an old woman who was busy sweeping her house. Finding out the three kings' destination, she asked them to wait for her. They said they

couldn't wait, but she could catch up with them. By the time the woman finished her cleaning, the kings were lost to sight. She is still searching for the Child, and on Twelfth Night she comes down the chimney with her broom to leave presents for the children, hoping that one will be the Christ Child.

From the Baptism and the marriage at Cana come the ingredients water, magic and the miraculous. The religious or sacred element is a continuing thread running through all three events and appears in all the celebrations.

In Greece the crucifix is cast into the sea and boys dive for it, the one who retrieves it receiving the priest's blessing for the year. In Florida there is the blessing of the sponge divers at Tarpon Springs. The beautiful ceremony begins with a mass in the church of St. Nicholas, continues with a magnificent procession of priests to the bayou where a white dove is released, symbolizing the Holy Spirit entering Jesus. Then the crucifix is cast into the water in memory of the Baptism, and the divers plunge to retrieve it.

In England, by the end of the fifteenth century, joy had taken the form of revel. The Saturnalian traditions were revived and became part of the Christmas celebration. The master of the revels was called The Lord of Misrule, that divine being whose ancestors were the Roman King of the Games and the King of the Winepots. The Lord of Misrule proclaimed a state of topsy-turvydom, where masters served servants and even kings submitted to his impudent orders. He was said to be responsible for the weather of the ensuing year by the spell he cast on each of the twelve days of Christmas, symbols of the twelve months.

With him appeared the mummers, players wearing masks and "keeping mum"—hence pantomime. They put on *pleyes* or *disports* (later sports) with dancing, music and jokes—an early form of our modern theater.

According to legend, it was Martin Luther, in the 1500s, who first decorated a Christmas tree. In spite of his austerity, stubbornness, and agonizing introspection, he was a cheerful man who loved music and good fellowship. He proclaimed Christmas as the time of joy.

But, incredibly, the Joy of Christmas was not a universally accepted idea. The literally "uptight" Puritans in England, responding to the long trail of Christmases right back to the Sat-

urnalia, regarded the festival as pagan. Finally on June 3, 1647, the Cromwellian Parliament announced that the feast of the Nativity of Christ and all religious festivals were out-lawed.

Our own Pilgrim Fathers copied the English laws and abolished Christmas. Along with plays (and mince pies) Christmas joined the list of things forbidden to "godly" men.

Oliver Cromwell was as bitter an enemy of Christmas as was King Herod, but Christmas has outlasted both. With the death of Cromwell in 1658, Christmas came out of hiding and took its place again in English and American life. The Lord of Revels will not be abolished, nor will Christmas, nor joy.

The feast on Twelfth Night takes many of its customs from celebrations of France, and also Germany and England. In England, a cake with a bean buried in it was a great feature of the feast. The bean king was he who had the good fortune to have the slice of cake in which was the bean.

A bean, a pea or a silver penny are the trinkets used to determine the monarch of the feast. The monarch, true to the centuries of tradition, chooses a whole court: a royal mate, a minister of state, maids of honor and ribald ladies of the bed-chamber. The hilarity and merriment is kindled by the Wassail. Games and pranks are part of the celebration. In England the nobility played cards and threw dice, and when tired of that they threw egg shells filled with rosewater at each other, or built elaborate castles and cannons of pasteboard and pelted and smeared them with claret during bloody dinnertime battles! Or they served large pies to naïve guests who lifted the lids —and out would hop live frogs!

I love dressing up and dancing and playing roles and games, and staging pranks. I've never done the live frogs, but it's fun to accumulate costumes and masks and have a dress-up room for those who like such things, with confetti and streamers, drums and noisemakers, magic tricks and games. Laughter is an ancient formula for the prevention and treatment of illness; the cultivation of imagination and creativity, a quality of health; and theater and games and playing and sport, important parts of man's life from as long ago as we can know.

Many years ago I read an article in *Gourmet* magazine that inspired me to celebrate Twelfth Night with a party proclaiming the end of the Christmas season and the coming of spring.

Menu
Feast of Twelfth Night

Harengs Frais Marinés

Roast Fresh Ham or
Choucroute au Champagne
Cappelletti Romagna

Mostarda di Frutta
Cakes
Pommes en Gelée

Lamb's Wool or Champagne

Harengs Frais Marinés
(Marinated Fresh Herring)

I buy marinated herring, but if there's time and if fresh herring is to be had, and if you know how to split and clean a fish, it's tempting to do it yourself.

Split and clean 2 pounds fresh herring and put them in ½ cup olive oil in a saucepan. In another saucepan bring to a boil 1¼ cups vinegar; 1 cup dry white wine; 2 medium onions and 1 carrot, both sliced; 4 sprigs of parsley, chopped; 6 peppercorns; and 1 bay leaf. Simmer the marinade until the onions and carrots are tender. Pour it over the herring and simmer the mixture for 15 minutes. Transfer the herring to a deep dish, cover them with the marinade, and chill them thoroughly. Arrange the fish in an hors-d'oeuvre dish, pour the marinade over them and garnish with slices of lemon.

Roast Fresh Ham

Sliver 5 garlic cloves and insert the pieces into slits made in a leg of pork. Into each incision put a bit of anchovy fillet. (I don't rub the roast with salt because of the salty anchovy fillet.) Rub the leg all over with a little oil and then some freshly cracked pepper. Roast it in a 325° F. oven for 25 to 30 minutes per pound, or until the meat thermometer reaches 165° F. (Insert the meat thermometer into the thickest part of the roast, not touching the bone.)

This is an excellent buffet dish. Roast the leg of pork in advance and let it settle at room temperature. It should be thinly sliced and goes well with pasta. The mustard fruit sauce is delicious with both this fresh ham and the Cappelletti. I served a roast fresh ham and a pasta with fresh basil sauce on a summer picnic.

Choucroute au Champagne
(Sauerkraut in Champagne)

Melt 4 tablespoons pork fat or lard in the bottom of a large heavy casserole or enameled pot. Sauté 2 large onions, sliced,

in the hot fat until they are transparent. Add the leaves from a sprig of fresh thyme or ½ teaspoon dried thyme; 2 bay leaves, crushed; and ¼ teaspoon freshly ground pepper. Pour in 1 bottle dry champagne and simmer the mixture slowly for 5 minutes. Add 4 pounds uncooked sauerkraut, a ½-pound piece of lean bacon, and ¼ pound lean salt pork. Cover the casserole and simmer the sauerkraut for 1 hour. Add 1½ pounds boneless shoulder of pork, sliced, and 1 pound boneless loin of pork. Cover the casserole and simmer the mixture for 3 hours. Ten minutes before serving, uncover the pot, add 6 frankfurters or garlic sausages, and cook the *choucroute* for 10 minutes without letting it boil.

Arrange the sauerkraut on a heated large platter, surround it and almost cover it with the bacon, sausages or frankfurters, and the pork, thickly sliced, and pour the sauce over all.

Choucroute is traditionally served with potatoes boiled or steamed in their jackets. For this feast I prefer the pasta.

Cappelletti Romagna

The Italians make a special and fabulous Twelfth Night pasta, naturally. (What is any day without pasta?) It is called Cappelletti Romagna, which means little Roman hats, and it is served with *mostarda di frutta,* candied fruits in a mustard sauce. Once a year is not enough for this rapturous creation.

Mix together 3 slices of prosciutto and ¼ pound cooked chicken, all chopped; 1 pound ricotta; 1 egg; 2 teaspoons grated Parmesan; and ¼ teaspoon each of black pepper and nutmeg. Roll out the dough for cappelletti and cut it into 2½-inch circles. Put 1 teaspoon filling in the center of each circle, fold the circles in half, enclosing the filling, and pull the edges together to give each the shape of a little dunce cap. Bring 2 quarts chicken broth or salted water to a boil and add the cappelletti. Cook them for 8 to 10 minutes, or until they are tender, and drain them carefully. Put them on a hot platter and serve with grated Parmesan and *mostarda di frutta.*

Dough for Cappelletti Sift 4 cups sifted flour onto a large pastry board, make a well in the center and add 3 eggs, lightly beaten. Add 2 teaspoons salt and mix the flour into the eggs, a

little at a time. Add, a few drops at a time, ¼ to ½ cup lukewarm water, or just enough to make the dough soft enough to knead. Flour the board and knead the dough with the heel of the hand for 10 to 12 minutes, or until it is smooth and elastic.

Mostarda di Frutta

(Candied Fruits in Mustard Sauce)

This is delicious with the Roast Ham as well as the Cappelletti.

Combine in a saucepan 1 cup sugar, ½ cup mustard seed and 1½ cups water. Bring the syrup to a boil and boil it rapidly for 5 minutes. Remove the syrup from the heat and let it stand for 12 hours, or overnight. Strain the syrup. Chop ¼ cup each of candied fruit as desired—citron, orange peel, grapefruit peel and cherries—and simmer the fruit in the syrup for 10 minutes. Cool and store.

Pommes en Gelée

(Jellied Apples)

Cut 8 to 10 apples and boil them with enough water to make 2 cups juice after draining. When the apples are very soft, drain them, reserving the juice, and discard the seeds and skins. Cool the pulp in the refrigerator as quickly as possible.

Combine in a saucepan 2 cups each of the reserved apple juice and sugar. Bring the liquid to a boil and boil the syrup until it sheets from a spoon, or a candy thermometer registers 219° F.

Mound the cold apple pulp on a glass serving dish. Pour the apple syrup on a plate a few inches larger than the inside of the plate holding the apple pulp. When the syrup has almost set into jelly, invert the plate over the mound of apple, completely covering it. Chill and serve very cold.

Sweets are a part of Twelfth Night feasts of all countries. Candied apples are in the highest tradition, as is a cake that the French call *gâteau des Rois.* In Paris the *gâteaux* are made from puff paste with a design crisscrossed on top, while in southern France they are made from a sweet yeast dough. In both places an almond, a bean or a tiny porcelain baby (!) is hidden in the cake; the person getting that slice is crowned king or

queen. The French custom of setting aside a piece to put by the door, *la part de Dieu,* for the first poor person who knocks is like the Greek custom of always leaving one bite on the dinner plate "for the stranger."

The Greeks hide a silver or gold coin in their cake to bring good fortune for the whole year to the one who finds it. The Dutch hide an almond in their bread; the finder is thought to be very wise and must bake another loaf! Like the French, the Mexicans hide a china doll or bean in the cake, and whoever finds it is not only king or queen of Twelfth Night, but must give a party for the same guests on El Dia de la Candelaria, February 2. This honor is not always welcomed and is avoided by swallowing the trinket.

Vasilopeta

(Greek New Year's Cake)

Soften 1 package of yeast in ¼ cup lukewarm water and dissolve it in ½ cup milk, scalded and cooled to lukewarm. Bring to a boil 2 cups milk and ¾ cup shortening, stir in ½ cup sugar and 1 teaspoon salt, and pour the mixture into a large mixing bowl. Let it cool until it is lukewarm. Stir in ½ teaspoon each of cinnamon and nutmeg; 3 eggs, unbeaten; and the dissolved yeast. Gradually add 5 to 6 cups flour to the liquid, beating the dough with the hand to blend, until it is thick but not dry.

Cover the bowl with a light towel and let the dough rise in a warm place for 1 hour. Turn the dough out on a lightly floured board and knead it down for a moment or two. Butter a round cake pan or a deep round mold and fill it half full with the dough. Insert a well-washed silver coin into the dough. Brush the top with melted butter, and let the dough stand in a warm place until it rises almost to the top of the pan. Brush the surface carefully with 1 egg yolk beaten with 1 tablespoon water, and sprinkle the dough with chopped almonds. Bake the cake in a moderate oven (350° F.) for 45 minutes, or until it is golden brown. Cool the cake on a rack, and make a cross of decorative frosting on the cake, using a pastry bag and tube or spoon.

Decorative Frosting Cream 2 tablespoons butter and gradually beat in 1 cup confectioners' sugar. Beat in slowly a few

drops of vanilla and enough heavy cream to make the icing easy to spread.

Lamb's Wool

Lamb's wool is the name of a traditional English drink used for Wassail, a toast that is offered around a large punch bowl. The word "Wassail" is derived from the Anglo-Saxon *Waas Hael,* meaning "What Hail!" and "Good Health!"

In England the Wassail Bowl used to be carried from door to door by villagers and good health was drunk to all. The bowl would be filled with as much as ten gallons of Lamb's Wool. Here is a recipe from the King's Royal Kitchen in 1633.

Boil three pints of ale, beat six eggs the whites and yolks together, set both on the fire in a pewter pot; add roasted apples, sugar, blanched almonds or beaten nutmeg; and cast on cinnamon, cloves and ginger; and being well brewed, drink it while hot.

Here is *Gourmet*'s recipe, which isn't that much different.

Steam or bake 4 large apples or 1½ pounds crab apples until they are tender. Press the pulp through a coarse sieve and discard the skins and seeds. Combine in a saucepan 1 quart brown ale, 1 pint sweet white wine, 1 cinnamon stick, ½ teaspoon ginger and ¼ teaspoon nutmeg. Heat the mixture slowly until it bubbles slightly, discard the cinnamon stick and pour the liquid over the apple pulp. Strain the lamb's wool through a fine sieve, pressing through as much of the pulp as possible. Heat it before serving, and sweeten with dark-brown sugar to taste.

Putting Things Away

Then everything settles, as it does in those glass-domed snow scenes that you shake and watch the snow fall and settle. In music there is a coda, "a passage at the end of a movement or composition that brings it to a formal close." The tree is disrobed and any broken and still fixable ornaments repaired, the lights checked and a note made in the red notebook about their condition and what is needed: new strings or bulb replacements. I wrap each ornament in a lot of tissue paper and pack them carefully into boxes—a chore, but I enjoy again the associations that each brings. The basement or attic is cleaned and all the boxes stored containing the wreaths, balls, crèches, animals, dolls, ornaments for next year's wreaths. The house is cleaned, the fruitcakes stored in tins and mincemeat put in a cool place, with reminders to give them both their drinks from time to time. And then I go to the florist and buy tulips and anemones and eucalyptus and amaryllis and give the house and myself a whiff of spring. But the memories of the winter solstice are wafting all about . . . an ending and a beginning.

I write things in the red notebook: ideas for next year, where things have been put and an admonition to myself on the first page of the next year's Christmas. Last year it was, "Don't get too tired . . . Enjoy it."

Some say that ever 'gainst that season comes
Wherein our Savior's birth is celebrated,
The bird of dawning singeth all night long:
And then, they say, no spirit dare stir abroad;
The nights are wholesome; then no planets strike
No fairy takes, nor witch hath power to charm,
So hallow'd and so gracious is the time.

SHAKESPEARE,
HAMLET

Bibliography

Baker, Margaret. *Christmas Customs and Folklore: A Discovering Guide to Seasonal Rites.* Princess Risborough and Aylesbury, England: Shire Publications, 1968.

Bock, Emil. *The Three Years: The Life of Christ Between Baptism and Ascension.* London: Christian Community Press, 1955.

Cate, Curtis. *Antoine de Saint-Exupéry, His Life & Times.* New York: G. P. Putnam's Sons, 1970.

Chang Chung-yuan. *Creativity and Taoism: A Study of Chinese Philosophy, Art & Poetry.* New York: Harper Colophon Books, 1970.

Derry, Evelyn Francis. *The Christian Year.* London: Christian Community Press, 1967.

Govinda, Lama Anagrika. *The Way of the White Clouds, A Buddhist Pilgrim in Tibet.* Berkeley: Shambala, 1970.

Gurdjieff, G. I. *All and Everything: Beelzebub's Tales to His Grandson, Books 1, 2, 3.* New York: E. P. Dutton, 1973.

Harrison, Michael. *The Story of Christmas, Its Growth and Development From the Earliest Times.* London: Odhams Press, n.d.

Heinlein, Robert. *Stranger in a Strange Land.* New York: Berkley Publishing, 1968.

Jaynes, Julian. *The Origin of Consciousness in the Breakdown of the Bicameral Mind.* Boston: Houghton Mifflin, 1977.

Jung, Carl. *Man and His Symbols.* Garden City, N.Y.: Doubleday, 1964.

Lao Tzu. *The Tao te Ching.* Translations and Commentaries: Wu, John C. H. Asian Institute Translation, No. 1. New York: St. John's University Press, 1961. Waley, Arthur. *The Way and its Power.* New York: Grove Press, 1958.
Chang Chung-yuan. *Tao: A New Way of Thinking.* New York: Harper Colophon Books, 1975.
Feng, Gia-Fu, and Jane English. New York: Vintage Books, 1972.

Lehner, Ernst and Johanna. *Folklore and Symbolism of Flowers, Plants and Trees.* New York: Tudor Publishing Company, 1960.

McCluggage, Denise. *The Centered Skier.* Waitsfield, Vt.: Vermont Crossroads Press, 1977.

Ram Dass, Baba. *The Only Dance There Is.* Garden City, N.Y.: Anchor Press, 1974.

Reich, Wilhelm. *Character Analysis.* New York: Random House, 1949.

————. *The Murder of Christ.* New York: Noonday Press, 1953.

Singer, June. *Androgyny: Toward a New Theory of Sexuality.* Garden City, N.Y.: Anchor Press, 1976.

Siu, R. G. H. *Ch'i, A Neo-Taoist Approach to Life.* Cambridge, Mass.: M.I.T. Press, 1974.

————. *The Man of Many Qualities: A Legacy of the I Ching.* Cambridge, Mass.: M.I.T. Press, 1968.

————. *The Tao of Science: An Essay on Western Knowledge and Eastern Wisdom.* Cambridge, Mass.: M.I.T. Press, 1957.

Spoerri, Daniel. *The Mythological Travels of a modern Sir John Mandeville, being an account of the Magic, Meatballs, and other Monkey Business Peculiar to the Sojourn of Daniel Spoerri upon the Isle of Symi, together with divers speculations thereon.* New York, by the Parking Lot of the Chelsea Hotel: Something Else Press, 1970.

Stone, Merlin. *When God Was a Woman.* New York: Dial Press, 1976.

Watts, Alan. *Tao: The Watercourse Way,* with collaboration of Al Chung-liang Huang. New York: Pantheon Books, 1975.

Whyte, Malcolm. *The Meanings of Christmas.* San Francisco: Troubadour Press, 1973.

Wilhelm, Richard, trans. *The I Ching, or Book of Changes.* Princeton, N.J.: Princeton University Press, 1967.

Wyckoff, James. *Wilhelm Reich: Life Force Explorer.* Greenwich, Conn.: Fawcett, 1973.

Index of Recipes

Alex and Nile's Sherbet *129*
Bear Claws *88*
Brandy Barnold *167*
Butter Cakes *85*
Cappelletti Romagna *182*
Chocolate Glaze *82*
Choucroute au Champagne *181*
Christollen *124*
Coconut Kisses *85*
Cranberry Salad *169*
Cranberry Sauce *129*
Creamed Vegetables: Leeks or Small Onions *127*
Crescents *85*
Date Surprises *85*
Dee's Greek Quince Sweet *38*
Dish of Snow *169*
Gin Alexander *124*
Harengs Frais Marinés *181*
Hazelnut Crescents *86*
Hella's Paté *79*
Jeannie's Grandmothers Fruit Soup *111*
Jeannie's Mother's Date-Nut Bars *89*
Jeannie's Persimmon Pudding *173*
Lamb's Wool *185*
Lebkuchen *83*
Linzer Cookies *88*
Maria's Eggnog *166*
Maria's Seville Marmalade *42*
Mashed Potatoes *126*
Mil's Oyster Stew *111*
Mimosas or Buckshots *167*
Mostarda di Frutta *183*
Mulled Wine *112*
My Father's Favorite Pear Preserves *44*
My Mother's Black Fruitcake *81*
Owl and the Pussycat's Chutney, The *41*
Paradise Jelly *43*
Pasta all'Arrabbiata *165*
Pastry Dough for the Mincemeat Pie *129*
Pear Chutney *41*
Pommes en Gelée *183*
Roast Fresh Ham *181*
Roast Pork with Sauerkraut *173*
Salads *165*
Schokolade Platzchen *84*
Soupirs aux Amandes *89*
Springerle *84*

Sugarplums 86
Swedish Ginger Snaps 86
Swedish Spritz 87
Thelma's Sweet Potato and Marshmallow Casserole 168
Tipsy Oregon Mincemeat Pie 78
Turkey and Oyster Pie 168
Turkey with Plain and Oyster Stuffing and Gravy 125
Turkey Soup 168
Vasilopeta 184
Vera's Sacher Torte 82
Vodka Frozen in Ice 125
White Fruitcake 80
Ya Ya's Sausages 79
Yin-Yang Candies 89